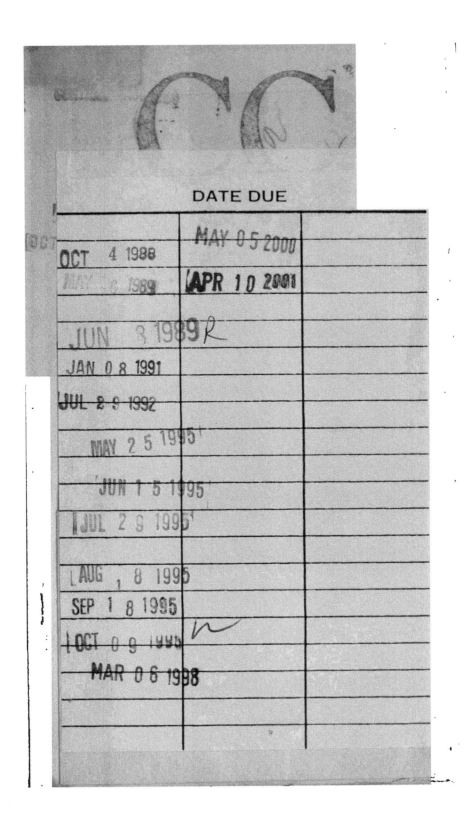

DATE DUE

OCT 4 1988	MAY 0 5 2000	
MAY 6 1989	APR 1 0 2001	
JUN 3 1989 R		
JAN 0 8 1991		
JUL 2 9 1992		
MAY 2 5 1995		
JUN 1 5 1995		
JUL 2 9 1995		
AUG 1 8 1995		
SEP 1 8 1995		
OCT 0 9 1995		
MAR 0 6 1998		

PELICAN BOOKS

A273

AN INTRODUCTION TO JUNG'S PSYCHOLOGY

FRIEDA FORDHAM

An Introduction to

JUNG'S PSYCHOLOGY

*

FRIEDA FORDHAM

PENGUIN BOOKS

BALTIMORE · MARYLAND

Penguin Books Ltd, Harmondsworth, Middlesex
U.S.A.: Penguin Books Inc., 3300 Clipper Mill Road, Baltimore 11, Md
AUSTRALIA: Penguin Books Pty Ltd, 762 Whitehorse Road,
Mitcham, Victoria

—

First published 1953
Reprinted 1954
Reprinted with revisions 1957
New edition 1959
Reprinted 1961, 1963

—

Made and printed in Great Britain
by Richard Clay & Company, Ltd,
Bungay, Suffolk
Set in Monotype Baskerville

CONTENTS

Editorial Note

BY C. A. MACE

Professor of Psychology, Birkbeck College

PSYCHOLOGICAL Pelicans are of two sorts. There is a general series which may be concerned with anything whatever of psychological interest – ranging from, say, Katz's *Animals and Men* to Zweig's *The British Worker*. The other sort has a more special purpose – to present the thought of the great psychologists in accordance with the principle 'Let the man speak for himself – or at least through an accredited interpreter'. In Margaret Knight's *William James*, James speaks in the main for himself. In the present volume Carl Gustav Jung speaks through a well accredited interpreter. This is the first of several volumes devoted to that kind of psychology commonly described in publishers' catalogues and elsewhere as 'psycho-analysis'.

The term 'psycho-analysis' is currently used to cover all those facts and theories presented in the works of Freud, Jung, and Adler, together with those of their associates, disciples, and intellectual heirs. It is so used despite persistent recommendations that it should be applied only to the theory and practice of Freud and his disciples, and that the theory and practice of Jung should be designated '*Analytical Psychology*', and that the theory and practice of Adler should be designated '*Individual Psychology*'. It will no doubt continue to be so used until someone suggests a new convenient title for the genus as distinct from the species.

'Psycho-analysis' in this broader sense covers both a set of theories and a set of practices. The most distinctive doctrine common to all the theories so described is that the mind, psyche, or personality of man comprises unconscious as well as conscious components, and that man's behaviour and his conscious states can be explained only by reference to the unconscious sources of motivation. What is common in the practice of the psycho-analytic schools (in the same broad sense of 'psycho-analytic') is the use of special techniques for bringing these unconscious factors into daylight. The techniques, like the theories, differ, but they are all sharply opposed to techniques which rely on drugs, hypnotic suggestion, or any other device not requiring the full and free cooperation of the subject to whom the technique is applied. The practice of psycho-analysis has grown out of, but is not restricted to, the treatment of

7

mental illness, and it is probably common ground to all the schools that the success of the treatment depends in the last resort upon the patient's own (assisted) self-diagnosis and his own (assisted) self-rehabilitation.

In one sense, the practice is prior to the theories, since the theories first emerged from facts brought to light in the therapeutic practice. These theories have, however, been extended and enriched by material derived from field anthropology, the study of mythologies and many other sources. As in all matters in which great human issues are involved controversy has been acute. There have been times when the sympathetic observer from outside might have experienced some anxiety lest scientific discussion should degenerate into a paltry sectarian squabble. But the danger, if it has not already passed, is quickly passing. In some respects both the theories and the practices of the schools continue to diverge, but there has also been a growth in tolerance and mutual understanding.

The different theories of the different schools meet different needs. A count of heads might well shew that the proportion of Jungians, Freudians, Adlerians, &c. would significantly vary in different sections of the educated public. A guess might be hazarded that those who found most enlightenment in the works of Jung were themselves largely of a certain caste or type of mind – a non-sectarian type of mind, a type disposed to those scientific studies which have a more intimate bearing on the larger humanities, and having a special interest in the most curious of curiosities of the human mind – symbolism, mythology, and religion – and yet not prone to dismiss their 'curiosities' as merely curious, and not disposed to catalogue all the literature of religion under the simple rubric of 'human illusions'. Such a finding would not be surprising, for Jung himself combines such a non-sectarian disposition with far ranging curiosities and far ranging sympathies. He, at any rate, bears no responsibility for sectarian squabbles. With characteristic modesty and characteristic tolerance, he is content to attribute much that is distinctive of his point of view not to innately superior insight, but to the influence of his own type and caste of mind.

In this Introduction, his thought is happily and appropriately presented by an interpreter who, like Jung himself, has no itch for partisan polemics, and no special interest in the less savoury curiosities of the unconscious mind, but a far ranging and quite insatiable curiosity in the varieties of human self-expression, whether such self-expression takes the form of some undatable mandala, a poem of Donne, or the latest deliverance of some contemporary

Editorial Note

mystic. The reader can enjoy all the attractive qualities of the introductory exposition with the added satisfaction of knowing that it is authentic. It has Jung's own *Imprimatur* and his personal commendation.

C. A. MACE

Foreword

BY DR C. G. JUNG

Mrs FRIEDA FORDHAM has undertaken the by no means easy task of producing a readable résumé of all my various attempts at a better and more comprehensive understanding of the human psyche. As I cannot claim to have reached any definite theory explaining all or even the main part of the psychical complexities, my work consists of a series of different approaches, or one might call it, a circumambulation of unknown factors. This makes it rather difficult to give a clear-cut and simple account of my ideas. Moreover, I always felt a particular responsibility not to overlook the fact that the psyche does not only reveal itself in the doctor's consulting-room, but above all in the wide world, as well as in the depths of history. What the physician observes of psychical manifestations is an infinitesimal part of the psychical world, and moreover often distorted by pathological conditions. I was always convinced that a fair picture of the psyche could only be obtained by a comparative method. But the great disadvantage of such a method consists in the fact that one cannot avoid the accumulation of comparative material, with the result that the layman becomes bewildered and loses his tracks in the maze of parallels.

The author's task would have been much simpler if she had been in possession of a neat theory for a *point de départ*, and of well-defined case-material without digressions into the immense field of general psychology. The latter, however, seems to me to form the only safe basis and measure for the evaluation of pathological phenomena, as normal anatomy and physiology are an indispensable precondition for their pathological aspect. Just as human anatomy has a long evolution behind it, the psychology of modern man depends upon its historical roots, and can only be judged by its ethnological variants. My works therefore offer innumerable possibilities of sidetracking the reader's attention with considerations of this sort.

Under those somewhat trying circumstances the author has nevertheless succeeded in extricating herself from all the opportunities to make mis-statements. She has delivered a fair and simple account of the main aspects of my psychological work. I am indebted to her for this admirable piece of work.

C. G. JUNG

Küsnacht/Zürich, September 1952

Biographical Sketch of C. G. Jung

CARL GUSTAV JUNG, the son of a pastor, was born in Kesswil (Canton Thurgau), Switzerland, on 26 July 1875. He was educated in Basel, where he took his medical degree, and in 1900 he began his career as a psychiatrist by becoming assistant at the Burghölzli Mental Hospital, Zürich, and the Psychiatric Clinic of Zürich University. He stayed there until 1909, with the exception of a short interval in 1902 when he studied under Janet in Paris, becoming in time senior staff physician, and working first as a student under, and later as a collaborator of, Eugen Bleuler. As a result of the research work he did there, using the new method known as the Association Tests, he published a number of papers, which made his name widely known, and brought him many invitations to lecture abroad, and in addition an honorary degree from Clark University (Massachusetts).

During this period Jung laid the foundations of the new interpretative psychiatry and also confirmed experimentally what Freud had already said. This led him naturally to champion Freud's work, and in 1907 they met personally – a meeting which led to friendship and several years of fruitful intellectual exchange between the two.

Jung became editor of Bleuler and Freud's *Jahrbuch für psychoanalytische und psychopathologische Forschungen,* and later (1911) first president of the International Psychoanalytic Society, which he himself founded.

Jung's individual lines of development had, however, been laid down from the start, and his criticism of Freud's theories in his book, *The Psychology of the Unconscious* ('Wandlungen und Symbole der Libido'), published in 1912, showed the difference in his conceptions from those of Freud, differences which led in 1913 to a final break with him and with the psychoanalytic school. Since then Jung's work has been known as Analytical Psychology, or sometimes as Complex Psychology. In 1909 Jung gave up his work at the Burghölzli in order to devote most of his time to scientific research along his own lines, writing, and the analysis of private patients, but he continued as instructor in Psychiatry at Zürich University until 1913, after which he devoted himself increasingly to research into the nature and phenomena of the unconscious, and the problems of psychological behaviour in general.

These researches eventually led him far afield in order to see and study for himself the behaviour and mental processes of primitive people. In 1921 he spent a considerable time in North Africa, and later among the Pueblo Indians in Arizona and New Mexico, and in 1926 he revisited Africa and lived among the natives who inhabit the slopes of Mount Elgon in Kenya. He also spent time in the United States of America, and visited India, England, and various European countries – visits which are reflected in many publications.

He gained much valuable material from the East, and also from contacts with scholars whose field of study it was, collaborating with Richard Wilhelm, who was a director of the China Institute in Frankfurt, and translator and commentator of most of the great works of Chinese philosophy and poetry. This work bore its fruit in 1930 in *The Secret of the Golden Flower*, published by Wilhelm and Jung. He also, later, co-operated with the German Indologist, Zimmer, whose last work (Zimmer died in 1943) Jung edited under the title of *Der Weg zum Selbst* (1944). A later collaboration was with the Hungarian mythologist Karl Kerényi, and resulted in two essays 'Das göttliche Kind' and 'Das göttliche Mädchen', published as a translation in one volume entitled *Essays on a Science of Mythology* by Jung and Kerényi.

Jung's own publications were many and varied. He was always a prolific writer, but comparatively few of his books have so far been translated into English, though a complete edition is now in progress and is being published simultaneously in Britain and America. His works have in addition been translated into nearly all European languages.

His scientific work, his wide interests, and his readiness to exchange ideas with others led to his becoming a leading personality in international research in the field of psychology. He was an excellent linguist (speaking four languages idiomatically and at least two others fairly well) and found no difficulty in responding to the many invitations which he received to lecture in other countries. In 1936 Harvard University, on the occasion of its tercentenary, awarded the most eminent living scientists honorary degrees, and Jung was one of this number. In 1938 he was given an honorary D.Sc. at Oxford University and was the first psychologist ever to receive such an honour in England. Many other degrees and honours were bestowed on him in the course of time, and in 1944 the University of Basel founded a chair of medical psychology specially for him, but he was unfortunately obliged to resign this within a year because of ill health. In 1930 he was given the honorary presidency of the Deutsche Ärztliche Gesellschaft für Psychotherapie and in 1933 the presidency of the International General Medical Society for Psychotherapy. Among the distinctions with which his native country honoured him were the Literary Prize of the City of Zürich (1932), the honorary membership of the Swiss Academy of Medical Sciences (1943), and the honorary doctorate of the University of Geneva (1945).

The story of Jung's development and career is, however, not so much that of a man collecting honours and filling important posts, but of an original mind and forceful personality, forging its own way, avoiding the well-trodden paths, and paying only the minimum dues to established conventions. That this led to clashes – as it did with Freud – was inevitable, but it also resulted in deep and enduring friendships, as the obituary notice on the death of Richard Wilhelm (published at the end of *The Secret of the Golden Flower*) shows.

Jung never sought followers, or tried to establish a system of thought which would attract large numbers. He believed in people experiencing and working things out for themselves whenever possible and always refused to be dogmatic. Almost in spite of himself, however, he founded a school of analysis, since inevitably many were drawn to his ideas, finding in them confirmation of their own experience, and explanation of what had hitherto been incomprehensible. For many years he held a seminar in Zürich which was conducted in English for the benefit of his many English-speaking students. After he retired from active work a training Institute was established there, known as the C. G. Jung Institute, which continues to give some of its teaching in English. There are also training Institutes in London and in San Francisco, and Jungian analysts practising all over the world.

He always had a great capacity for work, and in addition to his many activities in the psychological field, he found time to master a number of other subjects. He was a good classical scholar, had a vast knowledge of mythology and comparative religion, and was acquainted with the literature of many countries. He made contacts with important physicists, including the late Professor Pauli, the Nobel Prize winner, and found the gap between the two sciences – physics and psychology – narrower than one would have believed.

His wife, in her later years – after she had successfully brought up their one son and four daughters – was an active helper in his work until she died in 1955. She was a woman of intelligence and charm, who added her own contribution to his success. It is not easy to be the wife of a great man and preserve one's own identity, without over-emphasizing it, but she succeeded admirably in this, and was widely respected and loved. In addition to working as an analyst and lecturing in the Jungian Institute at Zürich she made a home which was a centre for visitors from all over the world, people of many different professions and a variety of interests, who gave Jung ample opportunity to keep in intimate touch with the movements and events of the times.

At one time Jung enjoyed many physical activities, including walking in his native mountains and yachting and swimming in the lake of Zürich. At eighty he had to give up these activities, but he still had a lively mind and continued to write books. He liked to talk, but he could listen too; he was in fact an excellent conversationalist with a memory for curious details and a fund of good stories and information about almost everything under the sun. He had a keen sense of humour, even of the mischievous, and was not averse to shocking anyone a little if they were too pompous or correct. He himself had no pretentiousness, there was no aura of the old wise man about him, though there were many who would have liked to see him in this light.

He said old age made him self-centred, but what struck one most about him was his humanity and kindliness, his lively interest in a host of things, and the continuing vitality of his unique personality.

He died in 1961.

CHAPTER I

Introduction

IN this chapter an attempt is made to give a simple outline of the psychology of C. G. Jung. To make such a simplification seems rather like drawing a map of the world on a sheet of paper: one conveys as little of the true nature of the psychology as of the seas and continents that make our globe. All the same, the map is a beginning, a framework in which later discoveries can be placed; if the outline seems blurred or confused, perhaps a later stage of the journey will make it clearer; and it is suggested that this first chapter shall be read in this light and returned to, if necessary, as the reader proceeds.

Jung's psychology is based firstly on his own experience with human beings, normal, neurotic, and psychotic. It is not a kind of psychopathology, though it takes the empirical material of pathology into account, but his theories are in his own words 'suggestions and attempts at the formulation of a new scientific experience with human beings'.[1] There is no simple formula to which this experience can be reduced; to focus on one point leads to a gain in clarity, but the network of relationships in which psychic activity consists is lost sight of. The search for precision in defining mental experience robs it of much that by nature belongs to it.

In speaking of mind and mental activity Jung has chosen the terms psyche and psychic, rather than mind and mental, since the latter are associated primarily with consciousness, whereas psyche and psychic are used to cover both consciousness and the unconscious. So-called unconscious phenomena are usually unrecognized by the one affected by them and have no connexion with the ego. If they do obtrude into consciousness – say, for instance, in the form of an emotional outburst that is out of proportion to its apparent cause – they

1. Foreword to *The Psychology of C. G. Jung* by Dr Jolande Jacobi.

15

are largely inexplicable to anyone who is unaware of the nature of unconscious motivation. 'I don't know what came over me', we say. Unconscious manifestations are not limited to the pathological, for normal people are continually acting from motives of which they are utterly unaware.[1]

The unconscious aspect of the psyche is different from, but compensatory to the conscious. In Jung's view the conscious mind 'grows out of an unconscious psyche which is older than it, and which goes on functioning together with it or even in spite of it'.[2] Furthermore, in contrast to those who look on mind as secondary manifestation, an epiphenomenon, 'a ghost in the machine', Jung insists on the reality of the psyche – it is no less real than the physical, has its own structure, and is subject to its own laws.

All that I experience is psychic. Even physical pain is a psychic event that belongs to my experience. My sense-impressions – for all that they force upon me a world of impenetrable objects occupying space – are psychic images and these alone are ... the immediate objects of my consciousness. My own psyche even transforms and falsifies reality, and it does this to such a degree that I must resort to artificial means to determine what things are like apart from myself. Then I discover that a tone is a vibration of the air of such and such a frequency, or that a colour is a wave-length of light of such and such a length. We are in all truth so enclosed by psychic images that we cannot penetrate to the essence of things external to ourselves. All our knowledge is conditioned by the psyche which, because it alone is immediate, is superlatively real. Here there is a reality to which the psychologist can appeal – namely, psychic reality.[3]

1. The evidence for the existence of the unconscious is now extensive; it is based on the study of the results of Association Tests, the psychoanalytic technique of Free Association, material derived from hypnosis, narcosis, dream analysis, &c., the study of such phenomena as dual personality, the functional disturbances, and the dissociation of mental and nervous disorders. It has not been thought necessary to include it here, but readers who are interested are referred to *The Spirit of Psychology* by C. G. Jung, Collected Works, Vol. 9.

2. 'Conscious, Unconscious, and Individuation', p. 281, Collected Works, Vol. 9, Part I.

3. *Modern Man in Search of a Soul*, pp. 219–20, 'Basic Postulates of Analytical Psychology'.

To this one may add that psychic reality forces itself upon us in many ways; there are even psychically produced illnesses which have all the appearance of being 'purely physical', and yet can be proved to have no organic cause, from the dramatic hysterical paralyses and blindness to headaches, stomach troubles, and a host of other minor ailments. Furthermore, everything made by man had its beginnings in the psyche, was something he just thought of, or perhaps saw in a dream or as a vision. Our own hopes and fears may be grounded in 'realities' that are recognizable to others, or they may be 'purely imaginary', but the joy or anxiety they bring is the same in either case – what we experience is real to us, if not to other people, and has its own validity, equal to, though different from, the 'reality' that is generally acknowledged.

This attitude towards the reality of the psyche contrasts strikingly with that to which Jung often refers as 'a nothing-but attitude'. Those who hold this point of view continually belittle psychic manifestations, especially experiences which cannot easily be connected with outside events, and refer to them disparagingly as 'nothing but imagination', or 'merely subjective'; Jung, on the other hand, gives the inner or psychic process a value equal to the outer or environmental one.

Jung's conception of the psyche is of a system which is dynamic, in constant movement, and at the same time self-regulating; he calls the general psychic energy libido.[1] The concept of libido must not be thought of as implying a force as such, any more than does the concept of energy in physics; it is simply a convenient way of describing the observed phenomena.

The libido flows between two opposing poles – an analogy might be drawn here with the diastole and systole of the heart, or a comparison made between the positive and negative poles of an electric circuit. Jung usually refers to the op-

1. The Latin word *libido* has by no means an exclusively sexual meaning (though it is frequently used in this way) but has the general sense of desire, longing, urge.

posing poles as 'the opposites'. The greater the tension between the pairs of opposites the greater the energy; without opposition there is no manifest energy. Many opposites at varying levels can be enumerated; for instance, progression, the forward movement of energy, and regression, the backward, consciousness and unconsciousness, extraversion and introversion, thinking and feeling, &c. The opposites have a regulating function (as Heraclitus discovered many hundred years ago), and when one extreme is reached libido passes over into its opposite.[1] A simple example of this is to be found in the way that an attitude carried to one extreme will gradually change into something quite different: violent rage is succeeded by calm, and hatred not infrequently turns in the end to liking. To Jung the regulatory function of the opposites is inherent in human nature and essential to an understanding of psychic functioning.

The natural movement of the libido is forwards and backwards – one could almost think of it as the movement of the tides. Jung calls the forward movement which satisfies the demands of the conscious, *progression*, the backward movement, satisfying the demands of the unconscious, *regression*. Progression is concerned with the active adaptation to one's environment, and regression with the adaptation to one's inner needs. Regression therefore (contrary to some points of view) is just as normal a counterpole to progression as sleeping is to waking, so long as the libido is functioning in an unhindered manner, i.e. according to the law of enantiodromia, when it must eventually turn over into a progressive movement. Regression may mean, among other things, a return to a dreamy state after a period of concentrated and directed mental activity, or it may mean a return to an earlier stage of development; but these are not necessarily 'wrong', rather can they be looked on as restorative phases –

1. 'Old Heraclitus, who was indeed a very great sage, discovered the most marvellous of all psychological laws: the regulative function of opposites ... a running contrariwise, by which he meant that sooner or later, everything runs into its opposite.' *Two Essays on Analytical Psychology*, p. 71.

'*reculer pour mieux sauter*'. If there is an attempt to force the libido into a rigid channel, or repression has created a barrier, or for one reason or another the conscious adjustment has failed (perhaps because outer circumstances became too difficult), the natural forward movement becomes impossible. The libido then flows back into the unconscious, which will eventually become over-charged with energy seeking to find some outlet. Perhaps the unconscious will then leak through into consciousness as fantasy, or as some neurotic symptom, perhaps it will manifest itself in infantile or even animal behaviour. It may even overwhelm consciousness so that there is a violent outburst, or a psychosis develops; when this happens it is as if a dam had burst and all the land was flooded. In extreme cases, where there is a complete failure of the libido to find an outlet, there is a withdrawal from life, as in some psychotic states; this is a pathological regression, and is unlike normal regression, which is a necessity of life. A man is not a machine who can continually and steadily adapt himself to his environment; he must also be in harmony with himself, i.e. adapt to his own inner world; 'Conversely, he can only adapt to his inner world and achieve unity within himself when he is adapted to the environmental conditions'.[1]

Libido is natural energy, and first and foremost serves the purposes of life, but a certain amount in excess of what is needed for instinctive ends can be converted into productive work and used for cultural purposes. This direction of energy becomes initially possible by transferring it to something similar in nature to the object of instinctive interest. The transfer cannot, however, be made by a simple act of will, but is achieved in a roundabout way. After a period of gestation in the unconscious a symbol is produced which can attract the libido, and also serve as a channel diverting its natural flow. The symbol is never thought out consciously, but comes usually as a revelation or intuition, often appearing in a dream.

1. *Contributions to Analytical Psychology*, p. 43, 'On Psychical Energy'.

As an example of this transfer of energy from an instinctive to a cultural purpose, Jung cites the spring ceremonial of the primitive Watschandis, who dig a hole in the earth, surround it with bushes in imitation of the female genitals, and dance round it holding their spears in front to simulate an erect penis. 'While dancing ... they thrust their spears into the ground and cry "Pulli nira, pulli nira, wataka!" (*Non fossa, non fossa, sed cunnus!*). During the ceremony none of the participants is allowed to look at a woman.'[1] The dance, which takes place in the spring, is charged with extraordinary significance. The dancers, through their movements and shouting, arouse themselves to an ecstasy; they are sharing in a magical act, the fertilization of the Earth woman, and other women are kept out of the way so that the libido shall not flow into ordinary sexuality. The hole in the earth is not just a substitute for female genitals, but a symbol representing the idea of the Earth woman who is to be fertilized, and is the symbol which transmutes the libido.

We should note here that throughout his work Jung uses the word 'symbol' in a definite way, making a distinction between 'symbol' and 'sign': a sign is a substitute for, or representation of the real thing, while a symbol carries a wider meaning and expresses a psychic fact which cannot be formulated more exactly. The Watschandis' hole in the earth can be looked on as a representation of a woman's genitals, but it also carries a deeper meaning; it is more than a sign, it is also a symbol.

There is a very close association between sexuality and the tilling of the earth among primitive people, while many other great undertakings, such as hunting, fishing, making war, &c., are prepared for with dances and magical ceremonies which clearly have the aim of leading the libido over into the necessary activity. The detail with which such ceremonies are carried out shows how much is needed to divert the natural energy from its course. This transmutation of libido through symbols, says Jung, has been going on since

1. *Contributions to Analytical Psychology*, p. 47, 'On Psychical Energy'.

the dawn of civilization, and is due to something very deeply rooted in human nature. In the course of time we have succeeded in detaching a certain proportion of energy from instinct and have also developed the will, but it is less powerful than we like to believe, and we still have need of the transmuting power of the symbol. Jung sometimes calls this the 'Transcendent Function'.

Jung's view of the unconscious is more positive than that which merely sees it as the repository of everything objectionable, everything infantile – even animal – in ourselves, all that we want to forget. These things, it is true, have become unconscious, and much that emerges into consciousness is chaotic and unformed, but the unconscious is the matrix of consciousness, and in it are to be found the germs of new possibilities of life. The conscious aspect of the psyche might be compared to an island rising from the sea – we only see the part above the water, but a much vaster unknown realm spreads below, and this could be likened to the unconscious.

The island is the ego, the knowing, willing 'I', the centre of consciousness. But what belongs to consciousness, what I know about myself and the world, and can direct and control, is not fully conscious all the time. I forget, or I repress what I do not like, or what is not socially acceptable. (*Repression* means a more or less deliberate and continuous withdrawal of attention, so that the thought, feeling, event, which is to be repressed is at last expelled from consciousness, and we are unable to recall it. *Suppression* – which is sometimes confused with repression – is the necessary withdrawal of attention from some things so that we can attend to others, but in this case they can be recalled at will.) I also have sense-perceptions of insufficient strength to reach consciousness, and I experience much that is only partly comprehended or of which I do not become fully aware. These subliminal perceptions, together with the repressed or forgotten memories, make a kind of shadow land stretching between the ego and the unconscious which could – in fact should – belong to the ego; or, to use our other metaphor, it is a land which has not always been covered by the sea, and can be reclaimed. Jung calls this shadow land the *personal* unconscious, to distinguish it from the collective unconscious, which is how he designates that aspect of the psyche which is unconscious in the fullest sense.

The personal unconscious belongs to the individual; it is formed from his repressed infantile impulses and wishes, subliminal perceptions, and countless forgotten experiences; it belongs to him alone.

The memories of the personal unconscious, though not entirely under the control of the will, can, when repression weakens (as for instance in sleep), be recalled; sometimes they return of their own accord; sometimes a chance association or shock will bring them to light; sometimes they appear somewhat disguised in dreams and fantasies; sometimes, especially if they are causing disturbances as in a neurosis, they need to be 'dug out'. Jung's method of arriving at these memories is analytic, and will be discussed later in some detail.

In the early stages of his work he also used what are known as 'Association tests'[1] to reach these memories. The association tests revealed a peculiarity of the psychic structure, namely the tendency of ideas to become associated round

---

1. *Contributions to Analytical Psychology*, pp. 262-3, 'The Psychological Foundations of Belief in Spirits'. 'The existence of complexes is easily demonstrated by means of the association experiment. This experiment consists in a very simple procedure: the experimenter calls out a word to the test-person, and the test-person immediately replies with the next association that comes into his mind. The reaction-time, i.e. the lapse of time between the stimulus word and the reply, is measured by a stop-watch. One would expect all simple words to be followed by an equally short reaction-time, and all difficult or rare words to cause a prolonged reaction-time. But as a matter of fact the reaction-times differ on this account far less than from other important reasons. Some very long reaction-times are produced unexpectedly by very simple stimulus words, and in the same case there may be no delay in replying to quite unusual stimulus words. Through careful examination of the test-person's individual psychology, I discovered that a prolongation of the reaction-time is usually due to interference by an emotion connected either with the stimulus word or with the reply. The emotion always depends upon the fact that the stimulus word has struck a complex.'

certain basic nuclei; these associated ideas – which are affectively toned – Jung named *complexes*. The nucleus is a kind of psychological magnet; it has energic value, and automatically attracts ideas to itself in proportion to its energy. The nucleus of a complex has two components, the dispositional and the environmental – i.e. it is determined not only by experience, but also by the individual's way of reacting to that experience.

A complex may be conscious, that is to say we know about it; or it may be partly conscious, in which case we know something of it, but are not fully aware of its nature; or it may be unconscious, in which case we are not aware of its existence at all. In both the latter cases, and especially when the complex is unconscious, it seems to behave like an independent person, and the ideas and affects centred round it will pass in and out of consciousness in an uncontrollable manner. Though it is somewhat artificial to make any sharp distinction when describing psychic contents, we can say that there are complexes which belong to the personal unconscious, and others which belong to the collective unconscious, a realm of the psyche that is common to all mankind.[1]

The collective unconscious is a deeper stratum of the unconscious than the personal unconscious; it is the unknown material from which our consciousness emerges. We can deduce its existence in part from observation of instinctive behaviour – instincts being defined as impulses to action without conscious motivation,[2] or more precisely – since there are many unconsciously motivated actions which are entirely personal and scarcely merit the term instinctive – an instinctive action is 'inherited and unconscious' and it is 'uniformly and regularly occurring everywhere'.[3] In-

1. To be strictly accurate some complexes belong to both realms. A mother complex for instance is personal insofar as it relates to our personal mother and collective in its relation to the archetypal mother.
2. *Contributions to Analytical Psychology*, p. 271, 'Instinct and the Unconscious'.
3. *Ibid.*, p. 273.

stincts are generally recognized; but not so the fact that, just as we are compelled to certain broad lines of action in specific circumstances, so also we apprehend and experience life in a way that has been determined by our history. Jung does not mean to imply by this that experience as such is inherited, but rather that the brain itself has been shaped and influenced by the remote experiences of mankind. But 'although our inheritance consists in physiological paths, still it was mental processes in our ancestors that created the paths. If these traces come to consciousness again in the individual, they can do so only in the form of mental processes; and if these processes can become conscious only through individual experience and thus appear as individual acquisitions, they are none the less pre-existing traces, which are merely "filled-out" by the individual experience. Every "impressive" experience is such an impression, in an ancient but previously unconscious stream-bed.'[1]

This tendency, one might say this necessity, to apprehend and experience life in a manner conditioned by the past history of mankind Jung calls archetypal, and archetypes are the 'pre-existent forms of apprehension' (i.e. existing before consciousness) or 'congenital conditions of intuition. ... Just as instincts compel man to a conduct of life that is specifically human, so the archetypes ... compel intuition and apprehension to forms specifically human.'[2]

Archetypes are unconscious, and can therefore only be postulated, but we become aware of them through certain typical images which recur in the psyche. Jung at one time spoke of these as 'primordial images' (an expression taken from Jacob Burckhardt), but later came to use the term archetype comprehensively to cover both the conscious and the unconscious aspects. Quite often in his writings he refers to archetype when strictly speaking he is meaning the archetypal image.

Jung thought that the archetypes were formed during the

1. *Contributions to Analytical Psychology*, p. 61, 'On Psychical Energy'.
2. *Ibid.*, pp. 275–6. 'Instinct and Unconscious'.

thousands of years when the human brain and human consciousness were emerging from an animal state but their representations, i.e. the archetypal images, while having a primordial quality, are modified or altered according to the era in which they appear. Some, especially those indicative of an important change in psychic economy, appear in an abstract or geometric form such as a square, circle, or wheel, either by themselves or combined in a more or a less elaborate way to form a typical and particularly important symbol. This will be discussed at length in a later chapter. Others present themselves as human or semi-human forms, gods and goddesses, dwarfs and giants, or they appear as real or fantastic animals and plants of which there are countless examples in mythology.

The archetypes are experienced as emotions as well as images and their effect is particularly noticeable in typical and significant human situations such as birth and death, triumph over natural obstacles, transitional stages of life like adolescence, extreme danger, or awe-inspiring experience. In these circumstances an archetypal image that might have been drawn in the caves of Auvergne will often appear in the dreams of the most modern of men.

The large question of dreams and dream interpretation will be dealt with in a later chapter, so that it must suffice to say here that Jung holds dreams to be natural and spontaneous products of the psyche, worth taking seriously, and producing an effect of their own, even if this is neither realized nor understood. Dream language is symbolic and makes constant use of analogies, hence its frequently obscure or apparently meaningless character.

The existence of the collective unconscious can be inferred in the normal man from the obvious traces of mythological images in his dreams – images of which he had no previous conscious knowledge. It is sometimes difficult to prove that no such knowledge ever existed (one can always say there was the possibility of cryptomnesia,[1]) but in certain kinds of

---

1. Cryptomnesia – something read, seen, or heard is forgotten and then later unconsciously reproduced.

mental disorder there is an astonishing development of mythological imagery which could never be accounted for by the individual's own experience.

Jung gives as one example of this the case of a patient in a mental hospital, in whom he was interested in the year 1906. The man was insane and was at times much disturbed, but in his quiet periods he described peculiar visions and produced very unusual symbolic images and ideas. It was not until 1910 that any light was thrown on these symbols, when Jung came across a Greek papyrus which had recently been deciphered and which dealt with similar material. As Jung says,

The vision of my patient of the year 1906, and the Greek text first edited in 1910, should be sufficiently separated for the possibility of a cryptomnesia on his side, and of thought transference on mine, to be excluded.[1]

Jung has spent much time in studying myths, for he considers them to be fundamental expressions of human nature. When a myth is formed and expressed in words, consciousness, it is true, has shaped it, but the spirit of the myth – the creative urge it represents, the feelings it expresses and evokes, and even in large part its subject-matter – come from the collective unconscious. Myths, it is true, often seem like attempts to explain natural events, such as sunrise and sunset, or the coming of spring with all its new life and fertility, but in Jung's view they are far more than this, they are the expression of how man experiences these things. The rising of the sun then becomes the birth of the God-hero from the sea. He drives his chariot across the sky, and in the west a great mother dragon waits to devour him in the evening. In the belly of the dragon he travels the depth of the sea, and after a frightful combat with the serpent of the night he is born again in the morning. These are widespread mythical themes which obviously reflect and can serve as ex-

1. *Contributions to Analytical Psychology*, pp. 108, 109, 'Mind and the Earth'.

planations of the physical process of the sun's rise and descent, but their emotional content makes them more than this. Primitive people do not differentiate sharply between themselves and their environment, they live in what Lévy-Bruhl calls *participation mystique*, which means that what happens without also happens within, and vice versa. The myth therefore is an expression of what is happening in them as the sun rises, travels across the sky, and is lost to sight at nightfall, as well as the reflection and explanation of these events.[1]

Because myths are a direct expression of the collective unconscious, they are found in similar forms among all peoples and in all ages, and when man loses the capacity for myth-making, he loses touch with the creative forces of his being. Religion, poetry, folk-lore, and fairy-tales, depend also on this same capacity. The central figures in all religions are archetypal in character, but as in the myth, consciousness has had a share in shaping the material. In primitive cults this is much less than in the higher and more developed religions, so that their archetypal nature is clearer. The most direct expression of the collective unconscious is to be found when the archetypes, as primordial images, appear in dreams, unusual states of mind, or psychotic fantasies. These images seem then to possess a power and energy of their own – they move and speak, they perceive and have purposes – they fascinate us and drive us to action which is entirely against our conscious intention. They inspire both creation and destruction, a work of art or an outburst of mob frenzy, for they are 'the hidden treasure upon which mankind ever and anon has drawn, and from which it has raised up its gods and demons, and all those potent and mighty thoughts without which man ceases to be man'.[2] The unconscious therefore, in Jung's view, is not merely a cellar where man dumps his rubbish, but the source of

1. For a development of this idea, and for examples of what *participation mystique* may mean in actual practice, the reader is referred to *Before Philosophy* by Henri Frankfort and others (Pelican Books).
2. *Two Essays on Analytical Psychology*, p. 66.

consciousness and of the creative and destructive spirit of mankind.

To attempt to define the collective unconscious is to attempt the impossible, for we can have no knowledge either of its boundaries or its true nature; all that we can do is to observe its manifestations, describe them, and try to understand them so far as is possible, and a large part of Jung's work has been devoted to this task. Of the archetypes he says, 'Indeed, not even our thought can clearly grasp them, because it never invented them'.[1] Nevertheless it has been possible to isolate various figures, which recur in dreams and fantasy series, which appear to have a typical significance for human beings, and which can be correlated with historical parallels and myths from all over the world; these Jung, after much careful research work, has described as some of the principal archetypes affecting human thought and behaviour, and has named the *persona*, the *shadow*, the *anima* and *animus*, the *old wise man*, the *earth mother*, and the *self*.

Here again we need to remember, when speaking of archetypes of the collective unconscious, that there are no watertight compartments in the mind, and that even the archetypes can have a personal aspect. The anima image, for instance, is conditioned both by the age-long experience men had of woman, and the actual personal experience a man has with a woman or women. Some archetypes are, however, more collective than personal, and others, like the persona and the shadow, have a larger personal element. This will become clearer when these archetypes are described in more detail, but first we must say something of Jung's work on the structure of the conscious mind.

1. *Ibid.*, p. 78. For a more comprehensive discussion of archetypes and the collective unconscious the reader is referred to *Contributions to Analytical Psychology*, and in particular the chapter 'Mind and the Earth'.

CHAPTER 2

Psychological Types

JUNG's contribution to the psychology of the conscious mind is largely embodied in his work on *Psychological Types*. The attempt to classify human beings according to type has a long history; it is nearly two thousand years since the Greek physician, Galen, tried to distinguish four fundamental temperamental differences in men, and his descriptive terms (though psychologically naïve) – the sanguine, the phlegmatic, the choleric, and the melancholic – have passed into common speech. There have been various attempts which, taking modern knowledge into account, aim at a more precise formulation – for instance, Kretschmer's – and Jung's division of people into extraverts and introverts has already come to be widely known, if not fully understood. Jung distinguishes two differing attitudes to life, two modes of reacting to circumstances which he finds sufficiently marked and widespread to describe as typical.

There is a whole class of men [he says] who at the moment of reaction to a given situation at first draw back a little as if with an unvoiced 'No', and only after that are able to react; and there is another class who, in the same situation, come forward with an immediate reaction, apparently confident that their behaviour is obviously right. The former class would therefore be characterized by a certain negative relation to the object, and the latter by a positive one ... the former class corresponds to the introverted and the second to the extraverted attitude.[1]

The extraverted attitude is characterized by an outward flowing of libido, an interest in events, in people and things, a relationship with them, and a dependence on them; when this attitude is habitual to anyone Jung describes him or her as an *extraverted type*. This type is motivated by outside factors

1. *Modern Man in Search of a Soul*, p. 98, 'Psychological Theory of Types'.

and greatly influenced by the environment. The extraverted type is sociable and confident in unfamiliar surroundings. He or she is generally on good terms with the world, and even when disagreeing with it can still be described as related to it, for instead of withdrawing (as the opposite type tends to do) they prefer to argue and quarrel, or try to reshape it according to their own pattern.

The introverted attitude, in contrast, is one of withdrawal; the libido flows inward and is concentrated upon subjective factors, and the predominating influence is 'inner necessity'. When this attitude is habitual Jung speaks of an 'introverted type'. This type lacks confidence in relation to people and things, tends to be unsociable, and prefers reflection to activity. Each type undervalues the other, seeing the negative rather than the positive qualities of the opposite attitude, a fact which has led to endless misunderstanding and even in the course of time to the formulation of antagonistic philosophies, conflicting psychologies, and different values and ways of life.

In the West we prefer the extraverted attitude, describing it in such favourable terms as outgoing, well-adjusted, &c., while the introverted attitude is dubbed self-centred and even morbid; on the other hand, in the East, at least until recent times, the introverted attitude has been the prevailing one. On this basis one may explain the material and technical development of the Western Hemisphere as contrasted with the material poverty but greater spiritual development of the East.

In *Psychological Types* Jung traces the influence of the two attitudes historically, as it affected the formulations of philosophy and the development of religion; he traces its effect on poetry, aesthetics, and lastly on psychology. In this view the difference between the 'psychological schools', especially those of Freud, Adler, and his own, rests on this difference in attitude. The Freudian attitude is extraverted, for it places the determinants of character upon outside people and events. The Adlerian attitude is introverted, for it emphasizes the significance of the inner attitude, 'the will to power'. The Jungian attitude may also be said to be introverted, since the factors in which Jung is most interested belong to the inner world, and especially to the 'collective unconscious'.

In attempting to divide human beings into recognizable types, Jung is dealing mainly with the psychology of consciousness; when a person is described as either extraverted or introverted, it means that his habitual conscious attitude is either the one or the other. A balanced attitude would include equally both extraversion and introversion, but it frequently happens that one attitude is developed and the other remains unconscious. No one, however, lives completely as one or the other, but manifests the unconscious attitude at times, though in an inferior way.

For instance, a man who is normally rather quiet and retiring – i.e. introverted – may show considerable activity and enthusiasm over something in which he is really interested, but still he will not be so well related to his surroundings as an extravert. He will chatter away about rare birds to someone who has not the remotest interest in them, or show a collection of ancient manuscripts to a bored guest who cannot understand what he sees in such rubbish.

The differentiation in attitude often seems to begin very early in life – in fact, there are grounds for considering that it may be innate. One may find both extraverted and introverted children in the same family, which is sometimes unfortunate for the latter type, who tend to be outshadowed by their sociable brothers and sisters.

The earliest mark of extraversion in a child is his quick adaptation to the environment, and the extraordinary attention he gives to objects, especially to his effect upon them. Shyness in regard to objects is very slight; the child moves and lives among them with trust. He makes quick perceptions, but in a haphazard way. Apparently he develops more quickly than an introverted child, since he is less cautious, and as a rule, has no fear. Apparently, too, he feels no barrier between himself and objects, and hence he can play with them freely and learn through them. He gladly pushes his undertakings to an extreme, and risks himself in the attempt. Everything unknown seems alluring.[1]

1. *Contributions to Analytical Psychology*, p. 303.

This is the type of child who is popular both with parents and teachers. He is spoken of as 'well adjusted', and is often considered 'brighter' than he really is because of his earlier development and his capacity to make a good impression.

The introverted child is shy and hesitant. He dislikes all new situations, and even approaches new objects with caution, and sometimes with fear. He prefers to play alone, and have one, rather than many friends. Because of the widespread preference for extraversion, such introverted children often cause anxiety to parents, but they are just as 'normal' and intelligent as the other type of child. They are thoughtful and reflective, and often have a rich imaginative life. What they need most is time to develop their less obvious gifts, and to learn to feel at home in the world.

The extraverted adult is sociable; he meets others halfway and is interested in anything and everything. He likes organizations, groups, community gatherings, and parties, and is usually active and on the whole helpful; this is the type that keeps our business and social life going. Extraverted intellectuals have similar qualities, and are at their best working with others, teaching or passing on their knowledge in some way; their good relationship with the world helps them to do this effectively.

Extraverts tend to be both optimistic and enthusiastic, though their enthusiasm does not last too well. The same is true of their relationships with other people, which are both easily and quickly made and broken.

The weakness of extraverts lies in a tendency to superficiality and a dependence on making a good impression; they enjoy nothing more than an audience. They dislike being alone, and think reflection morbid, and this, together with a lack of self-criticism, makes them more attractive to the outer world than to their family or immediate circle, where they can be seen without disguise. Since they are well adapted to society, they usually accept the morals and convictions of the day, and so tend to be somewhat conventional in their judgements; but they are nevertheless most useful people and absolutely necessary to any communal life.

Introverted adults, on the other hand, dislike society and feel lonely and lost in large gatherings. They are sensitive and afraid of looking ridiculous, but they often seem unable to learn how to behave in social situations: they are clumsy, or they are too outspoken, or they are scrupulously and rather ridiculously polite. They tend to be over-conscientious, pessimistic, and critical, and always keep their best qualities to themselves, so that naturally they are easily misunderstood.

Since they can only show their gifts in sympathetic surroundings, they tend to be overlooked, and consequently are less successful than their extraverted colleagues; yet, because they do not spend their energy trying to impress others, or dissipate it in social activities, they may often possess unusual knowledge, or have developed some talent above average standards.

Introverted people are at their best when alone, or in a small and familiar group; they prefer their own thoughts to conversation and books, and quiet pursuits to noisy activity. Their own judgement is more important to them than a generally accepted opinion – an introvert will put off reading a book that is popular and depreciate anything that is widely acclaimed. This independence of judgement and lack of conventionality can be valuable if rightly understood and used, and in spite of their lack of social graces they often make loyal and sympathetic friends.

Unfortunately the two types misunderstand one another and tend to see only the other's weakness, so that to the extravert the introvert is egotistical and dull, while the introvert thinks the extravert superficial and insincere.

It is clear that these differences in attitude can cause misunderstandings and difficulties in marriage, yet, strangely enough, there is a marked tendency for either type to marry its opposite. Each secretly hopes that the other will take care of the side of life they find uncongenial; the quiet, thoughtful man finds a lively, practical wife, who arranges the social activities that further his business or professional career, and the shy, withdrawn woman attracts a husband who is only

B

too glad to leave his wife safely at home while he immerses himself in the world. All goes well so long as their chief concern lies in adapting themselves to the many needs of life, establishing a career, building up a family, and making a secure financial position. If they are content to remain at this level theirs may be (at least outwardly) an ideal marriage, but if they look for real understanding or a fuller companionship difficulties will arise – 'Each speaks a different language. The value of the one is the negation of value for the other'.[1]

They become critical of each other's interests (or so-called lack of interest) and of each other's friends; one tries to push the other into activity, or complains bitterly of the restlessness of the partner; each feels misunderstood, and may give way to self-pity or look for someone else who will have the necessary sympathy and understanding – or at least an appearance of it. Imperceptibly the rift widens and the two types begin to be ranged in opposition to one another.

Sometimes toleration, and an attempt to recognize the values of the other, will bridge the gap, at least for a time, but often a violent and poisonous warfare results, even if, as Jung remarks, conducted in the utmost intimacy.[2] The real solution of this problem lies in a far-reaching development of each personality, which can in many cases only be brought about with psychological help.

In making the distinctions between extravert and introvert one does not cover all the differences in personality that can be observed. The introvert draws back and hesitates in a definite way, not necessarily in the manner of every other introvert. The extravert makes his relationship with the world through his intellect, his feelings, his sense-perceptions, or his intuitions. Each in the struggle for existence instinctively uses what Jung calls his 'most developed function'.[3]

1. *Two Essays*, p. 54.
2. *Ibid.*, p. 101.
3. 'Just as the lion strikes down his enemy or his prey with his forepaw, in which his strength resides, and not with his tail like the crocodile, so our habitual reactions are normally characterized by the applica-

There are four functions, he considers, which we use to orientate ourselves in the world (and also to our own inner world): *sensation*, which is perception through our senses; *thinking*, which gives meaning and understanding; *feeling*, which weighs and values; and *intuition*, which tells us of future possibilities and gives us information of the atmosphere which surrounds all experience.[1]

When a reaction is habitual one may speak of a type. For example, there are people who obviously think more than others, who use their thought in making decisions, who like to think things out, and who regard thought as the most important attribute of human beings. These people may be either extraverted or introverted, and this will influence the manner and the subject-matter of their thought. The direction of the extraverted thinker's thought is towards the outside world. He is interested in facts and material, and if he is concerned with ideas they will be derived either from tradition or from the atmosphere of the time; they will arise from what is generally known as 'reality'. This is what is usually recognized as thinking, and yet, as Jung points out, there is another kind of thought to which the term can hardly be denied.

I reach this other kind of thinking in the following way. When my thoughts are engaged with a concrete object or general idea in such a way that the course of my thinking eventually leads me back again to my object, this intellectual process is not the only psychic proceeding taking place in me at the moment. I will disregard all

tion of our most trustworthy and efficient function; it is an expression of our strength. However, this does not prevent our reacting occasionally in a way that reveals our specific weakness. The predominance of a function leads us to construct or to seek out certain situations while we avoid others, and therefore to have experiences that are peculiar to us and different from those of other people.
'An intelligent man will make his adaptation to the world through his intelligence, and not in the manner of a sixth-rate pugilist, even though now and then, in a fit of rage, he may make use of his fists.' *Modern Man in Search of a Soul*, p. 101.

1. *Psychological Types*, p. 568. (Intuition, says Jung, is perception via the unconscious.)

those possible sensations and feelings which become noticeable as a more or less disturbing accompaniment to my train of thought, merely emphasizing the fact that this very thinking process which proceeds from objective data and strives again towards the object stands also in a constant relation to the subject. This relation is a *conditio sine qua non*, without which no thinking process whatsoever could take place. Even though my thinking process is directed, as far as possible, towards objective data, nevertheless it is *my* subjective process, and it can neither escape the subjective admixture nor yet dispense with it. Although I try my utmost to give a completely objective direction to my train of thought, even then I cannot exclude the parallel subjective process with its all-embracing participation, without extinguishing the very spark of life from my thought. This parallel subjective process has a natural tendency, only relatively avoidable, to subjectify objective facts, i.e. to assimilate them to the subject.

Whenever the chief value is given to the subjective process, that other kind of thinking arises which stands opposed to extraverted thinking, namely, that purely subjective orientation of thought which I have termed introverted. A thinking arises from this other orientation that is neither determined by objective facts nor directed towards objective data – a thinking, therefore, that proceeds from subjective data and is directed towards subjective ideas or facts of a subjective character.[1]

To say an idea is subjective is often used as a term of reproach, but this is to overlook the fact that no thought is possible without the thinker and that his share in it is responsible for its ultimate shape.

The merits of extraverted thinking – namely, its 'down-to-earth nature', its concentration on objects, and the discipline that this imposes – is at the same time its limitation; it becomes all too easily tied to facts; it cannot see beyond them, or free itself for the purpose of establishing an abstract idea. It becomes clogged by a mass of undigested material, and tries to escape from this dilemma by artificial simplifications – by inventing formulae and concepts which appear to give coherence to what is really disconnected.

A creative thinker like Charles Darwin, who is an excellent example of an extraverted thinker, could give order and

1. *Psychological Types*, pp. 430–1.

meaning to the mass of facts he collected, but where the creative idea is lacking the thinker compensates by producing more and more facts, until there is a mountain of material, often of doubtful value.

When the life of an individual is mainly ruled by thinking and his actions are usually the result of an intellectually considered motive, he may fairly be called a *thinking type*. The pure type is more often found among men than among women, whose thinking is usually of an intuitive nature. This type 'thinks things out' and comes to conclusions based on objective data – what he calls 'the facts'. He likes logic and order, and is fond of inventing neat formulae to express his views. He bases his life on principles and would like to see others do the same. Wherever possible his family, his friends, and his working associates are included in his 'scheme of living', and he has a strong tendency to believe that his formula represents absolute truth, so that it becomes a moral duty to press its claims. This can lead him into equivocal situations through assuming that 'the ends justify the means'. He believes that he is rational and logical, but in fact he suppresses all that does not fit into his scheme, or refuses to recognize it. He both dislikes and fears the irrational, and he represses emotion and feeling, and tends to become cold and lacking in understanding of human weakness. He neglects the art of friendship and of relationship to other people, and is often a family tyrant. He can sacrifice his friends and family to his principles without the least idea that he is doing so – it is all for their good. This type of man tends to have unfortunate love affairs, as his repressed feelings are likely to burst out with a violence beyond his control and to attach themselves to unsuitable women. In addition, he suffers from irrational moods which he does not admit, and doubts about his beliefs which he stifles with fanaticism. He often has a strong sense of duty, and his formula for life may include much that is good, even noble, but his manner of putting it into practice will lack warmth, tolerance, and those human qualities that refuse to be fitted into schemes and formulae.

37

His thinking, however, is positive – it produces something, either new facts or new conceptions.

Even when it analyses, it constructs, because it is always advancing beyond the analysis to a new continuation ... It is, in any case, characteristic that it is never absolutely depreciatory or destructive, but always substitutes a fresh value for one that is demolished. This quality is due to the fact that thought is the main channel into which a thinking type's energy flows.[1]

In contrast to the extravert, the introverted thinking type is not interested in facts but in ideas; the chief value of this type of thinking lies in the new view it presents.

Jung says of introverted thinking:

External facts are not the aim and origin of this thinking, although the introvert would often like to make it so appear. ... It formulates questions and creates theories; it opens up prospects and yields insight, but in the presence of facts it exhibits a reserved demeanour. As illustrative examples they have their value, but they must not prevail. Facts are collected as evidence or examples for a theory, but never for their own sake ... its actual creative power is proved by the fact that this thinking can also create that idea which, though not present in the external facts, is yet the most suitable abstract expression of them.[2]

The introverted thinking type is interested in the inner, not the outer reality. What is important to him is the development and presentation of the 'primordial image' and its shaping into an idea. This has for him a compelling power; he has a vague notion that the idea may be of use to the world, sometimes even a conviction that it would be saved if it only knew, but these are secondary considerations, and not of vital importance to him.

The introverted thinker viewed from outside is usually a distinctly odd character. Because of his concern with inner realities he gives little or no attention to his relationships with the world. He does not notice what is going on or understand how other people think or feel; he is either shy and silent in their company or else makes some inappropriate remark.

1. *Psychological Types*, p. 442.   2. *Ibid.*, pp. 480–1.

The absent-minded professor is the typical example of an introverted thinker. An amusing story of the philosopher Schopenhauer illustrates the characteristics well: it is said that he was standing lost in thought in the middle of a flower-bed in a city park, when a gardener shouted to know what he was doing, and who did he think he was? 'Ah!' said Schopenhauer, 'if only I knew the answer to that!'[1]

The weakest point in both the thinking types is their neglected and under-developed feeling function. To understand what Jung means by feeling, one needs to make a distinction between the different ways in which the word can be used: feeling hot or cold is a sense-impression; feeling that something will happen, that someone is deceiving you (or having any similar experience) refers to a 'hunch' or intuition; when, however, one says 'I feel sorry' or 'I feel that is bad' or 'good', one is making a valuation of an emotionally toned experience. It is in this sense that Jung uses the word feeling when he speaks of a 'feeling function'.

When we think, it is in order to judge or to reach a conclusion, and when we feel it is in order to attach a proper value to something.[2]

Feeling is often confused with emotion – in fact, Jung himself sometimes talks of the two together almost as if they were the same thing, but when he does make it clear he says explicitly that *any* function can lead over into emotion, and the emotion itself is not the function. Neither is feeling a kind of muddled thinking, as the thinking type is inclined to believe; it is the function by which values are weighed, accepted, or refused.

Jung speaks of both 'feeling judgements' and 'feeling situations'; the realm of feeling includes the two, but in the latter case one is nearer the emotional end of the scale, though the valuing element enters in too. In a 'feeling situation' one values, i.e. judges the atmosphere and behaves

1. 1936 Seminar (privately circulated).
2. *Modern Man in Search of a Soul*, p. 105, 'Psychological Theory of Types'.

accordingly. Women are usually adept at this, but there are also men who are feeling types. They function best in situations where personal relationships are important; intermediaries of every sort from diplomats to salesmen need to have well-developed feeling.

Feeling and thinking are inimical to each other. 'In science where thinking is the main function ... the lowest microbe has to be granted the same concentration as the sun.'[1] But feeling disapproves of this, and insists on the difference in their values being recognized.

Feeling is a rational function; one does not normally feel that a thing is valuable one moment and worthless the next; feeling types have an ordered scheme of things, a hierarchy of values to which they hold, and a strong sense of history and tradition. It is a discriminating function, and where there is little or no feeling you find – as in an extreme example of extraverted thinking – a tremendous accumulation of facts, some of value and others completely worthless.

Feeling is specially concerned with human relationships, and with the value (or lack of value) of people, and their modes of behaviour towards one another. It is not surprising, therefore, that it is an important element in many religions, and especially in both Christianity and Buddhism.

When feeling has priority over the other functions, one can speak of a feeling type, and when the type is extraverted, feeling will be governed by and adjusted to the environment; this type is more often found among women than among men.

The extraverted feeling type is well adjusted to the world, valuing on the whole what is generally valued and finding no difficulty in fitting in with her time and *milieu*. This is particularly noticeable when she marries, for she always chooses such an eminently suitable husband that one might well think she had planned it all, but in fact she falls in love quite genuinely with the 'right' kind of man.

She is specially concerned with personal relationships and has often tact and charm, smoothing awkward situations and

1. 1936 Seminar (privately circulated).

40

pouring oil on troubled waters; and it is she who makes social and family life possible. She is naturally a good hostess, and is thoroughly at home in groups, large gatherings, and every social and communal activity. The feeling type who becomes aware of unhappiness or injustice has usually a real desire to help, and a great deal of excellent social work is based on this function. At best she is sympathetic, helpful, and charming; at worst superficial and insincere. So long as her feeling remains personal it is genuine, but if it is pushed to extremes it becomes unrelated and artificial, losing its original human warmth, and giving an impression of pose and unreliability.

Introverted feeling is governed by subjective factors, and the type is outwardly very different from the warm, friendly extravert, often giving an impression of coldness; but the feeling in reality gathers intensity with its lack of expression, and one may truly say of this type that 'still waters run deep'. Whilst appearing reserved, they have usually much sympathy for and understanding of intimate friends, or anyone suffering or in need. In a woman of this type feeling often flows secretly into her children; she is not demonstrative, but has all the same a passionate love that will become apparent if the child is seriously ill, or if she is separated from it in some way. Introverted feeling also expresses itself in religion, in poetry and music, and occasionally in fantastic self-sacrifice.

The introverted feeling type is unadaptable. He or she is disconcertingly genuine, and if ever forced to play a role, is likely to fall to pieces, for this reason being sometimes described as schizoid. But in intimate circles to which they are attached by strong emotional ties their value is well known, and they make constant and reliable friends.

What Jung means by feeling is often misunderstood; there is no doubt what he means by sensation: it is that which reaches us through the senses. As sense-perception sensation is dependent upon the object causing the sensation, and also upon the recipient. In the former case – i.e. where the emphasis is on the object – the sensation is said to be extraverted. When sensation has priority, instead of merely seconding another function, we can speak of a sensation type. In this type no objective sensation is excluded; in other types, especially the intuitive, much that is sensed scarcely reaches consciousness; intuitives, for instance, often forget they have a body – they feel they could almost fly.

The sensation type takes everything as it comes, experiences things as they are, no more and no less; no imagination plays around his experiences, no thought attempts to look deeper into them or explore their mysteries – a spade is a spade; neither is any real valuation made; what counts is the strength and pleasure of the sensation.

This type is therefore irrational; there is little logic in the experience of the senses, and even the same thing may arouse a different sensation at different times. They are often, however, mistakenly thought to be rational, since their insistence on facts and their calm, even phlegmatic natures, give a false impression of reasonableness. Sensation types are frequently easy, jolly people with a great capacity for enjoyment, but their danger lies in an over-valuation of the senses, so that they may degenerate into unscrupulous sybarites, or restless pleasure-seekers forever looking for new thrills.

When the type is extraverted the object arousing the sensation is the important thing, when introverted the sensation experienced is more important, and objects are secondary, or even do not count at all. Many artists and musicians are examples of the latter type; contemporary art, with its high degree of subjectivity, springs from introverted sensation with an admixture of feeling.

Most introverted sensation types, suffering from the characteristic introverted difficulty in expressing themselves, are very difficult to understand. They are overwhelmed by impressions and need time to assimilate them, and are often preoccupied with images from the collective unconscious. Even precise observation of reality does not stop the subjective factor from working – such people cannot see buses or trams without thinking of fiery dragons, trees have faces, and inanimate objects spring to life; they think they see people who are not really there, and have curious experiences with 'ghosts'.

The opposite function to sensation is intuition, though, like sensation, it is an irrational function. 'Intuition,' says Jung, 'is a perception of realities which are not known to consciousness, and which goes via the unconscious.' It is more, however, than a mere perception, for it is an active creative process which seizes upon the situation and tries to alter it according to its vision. It has the capacity to inspire, and in every 'hopelessly blocked situation [it] works automatically towards the issue which no other function could discover.'[1] Whenever a judgement or a diagnosis has to be made in the dark intuition comes into play. Scientists and physicians, inventors, certain classes of business men and politicians, judges and generals all must make use of this faculty at times, and of course ordinary people as well.

Whenever strange conditions have to be dealt with, or situations met where established values and concepts do not work, then intuition must be brought into play.[2]

The extraverted intuitive type lives mainly through this faculty of intuition; the important things are all possibilities. He or she dislikes intensely anything that is familiar, safe, or well-established. He is no respecter of custom, and is often ruthless about other people's feelings or convictions when he is hot on the scent of something new; everything is sacrificed for the future. Neither religion nor law is sacrosanct, so that he often looks like a ruthless adventurer; but he has in fact his own morality based on loyalty to his intuitive view. For him not to 'take a chance' is simply cowardly or weak.

The danger to this type of man is that he sows but never reaps. He squanders his life in possibilities while others enjoy the fruits of his energy and enterprise. It is almost impossible for him to carry a thing through to the end, or at least beyond the point where its success is established. Naturally his

1. *Psychological Types*, p. 463.
2. 1936 Seminar (privately circulated).

personal relationships are very weak; he finds it difficult to stick to one woman, and home soon becomes a prison. On the other hand, as the wife of such a man once said, life with him is never dull.

The extraverted intuitive is concerned with what is commonly known as the world of reality; the introverted intuitive is concerned with the collective unconscious, the dark background of experience – all that is subjective, strange, and unusual to the extravert.

The peculiar nature of introverted intuition, when given the priority ... produces a peculiar type of man, viz. the mystical dreamer and seer on the one hand, or the fantastical crank and artist on the other. The latter might be regarded as the normal case, since there is a general tendency of this type to confine himself to the perceptive character of intuition. As a rule, the intuitive stops at perception; perception is his principal problem, and – in the case of a productive artist – the shaping of perception. But the crank contents himself with the intuition by which he himself is shaped and determined.[1]

This is the type that sees visions, has revelations of a religious or cosmic nature, prophetic dreams, or weird fantasies, all of which are as real to him as God and the Devil were to medieval man. Such people seem very peculiar to-day, almost mad, as in fact they are, unless they can find a way to relate their experiences with life. This means finding an adequate form of expression, something collectively sanctioned, not just a living out of fantasies. They can sometimes do this by finding, or even forming a group where their vision is of some value. In primitive communities these people have value and command respect – they are of the stuff from which the prophets of Israel were fashioned – but except as mystics in religious communities there is little place for them in the world of to-day. Usually they keep quiet about their experiences, or form esoteric sects or little groups concerned with 'other world experience'. Ordinarily they seem rather odd, and quite harmless, but if gripped by their inner vision

1. *Psychological Types*, p. 508.

they may become possessed by a force which is powerful for good or evil, and is highly contagious: both religious conversion and mob violence start in this way.

As a rule, the intuitive contents himself with perception, and if he happens to be a creative artist, with the shaping of perception; he will paint 'in iridescent confusion, embracing both the significant and banal, the lovely and the grotesque'. William Blake is a good example of an introverted intuitive who was both artist and poet.

Since human nature is by no means simple, one rarely finds the absolutely pure type; often the main function is sufficiently clear to dub the person a thinker, an intuitive and so on, but it is seconded by another function which modifies and blurs the picture. Jung in fact refers to his description of types as 'somewhat Galtonesque family portraits', for human nature refuses to be classified in a precise and simple way. All the same, the concept of types has great practical value as an aid to understanding in personal relationships and in education. It is of help to husbands and wives to realize that their partner 'works' in a different way and is not simply being obtuse, to teachers to realize that an introverted child, for instance, is not unhappy or unadapted if it does not join in activities with the same zest as extraverted pupils, and to the psychotherapist in treating his patient. It is very common among neurotic people to have developed one function to such perfection that the others are perforce neglected; intuitives, for instance, usually neglect sensation, and consequently their own bodies, so that they may become physically ill; thinking types neglect feeling, and so get into serious trouble where personal relationships are important. Mental (and sometimes physical) health therefore depends on the development of the neglected function, so that the personality may become more nearly whole.

Most people use one function (or its modification), more complicated people use two functions, and a very highly differentiated personality would make use of three functions. The inclusion of the fourth function belongs to what Jung has called the individuation process, and the reconciliation of the opposing trends of one's nature; but to understand what is meant by this we must first consider Jung's concepts of the personal and collective unconscious in more detail.

CHAPTER 3

Archetypes of the Collective Unconscious

THE development of an attitude, either extraverted or introverted, and a function, is part of the process of living, of
adapting ourselves to our world and making our mark in it.
Unless there is some strong interference, we develop along
the lines that are easiest to us, but we also like to 'put our
best foot foremost'. This means that we usually develop our
best function, be it thinking or intuition, feeling or sensation,
and at the same time have a strong tendency to conform to
what is expected of us, to respond to education and social
pressure, to behave in an accepted way. In this process much
that rightly belongs to the personality is lost, or rather it is not
lost but has simply been pushed away into unconsciousness;
in psychological terms it has been repressed. Small children
left to behave naturally are often lustful, acquisitive, and
aggressive, and show all the tendencies that the adult is sup-
posed to have grown or been educated out of. But the mistake of most educators, parents, teachers, and others, is to
believe that they have really changed the nature of the children in their care, while all that has happened is that the
disagreeable or inferior tendencies have been pushed into
the background and forgotten, yet live on in the adult. This
forgetting is often so successful that we come to believe that
we are exactly as we appear to be, sometimes with disastrous
results. These repressed tendencies belong to what Jung calls
the personal unconscious, and far from withering away, as
one might hope, they seem to be like neglected weeds that
flourish in any forgotten corner of the garden.

The process of civilizing the human being leads to a com-
promise between himself and society as to what he should
appear to be, and to the formation of the mask behind which
most people live. Jung calls this mask the *persona*, the name
given to the masks once worn by the actors of antiquity to

signify the role they played. But it is not only actors who fill a role; a man who takes up a business or a profession, a woman who marries or chooses a career, all adopt to some extent the characteristics expected of them in their chosen position; it is necessary to do so in order to succeed. A business man will try to appear (and even to be) forceful and energetic, a professional man intelligent, a civil servant correct; a professional woman nowadays needs not only to appear intelligent but also well dressed, and a wife is required to be a hostess, a mother, a partner, or whatever her husband's position demands.

Society expects, and indeed must expect, every individual to play the part assigned to him as perfectly as possible, so that a man who is a parson ... must at all times ... play the role of parson in a flawless manner. Society demands this as a kind of surety: each must stand at his post, here a cobbler, there a poet. No man is expected to be both ... that would be 'queer'. Such a man would be 'different' from other people, not quite reliable. In the academic world he would be a dilettante, in politics an unpredictable quantity, in religion a free-thinker – in short he would always be suspected of unreliability and incompetence, because society is persuaded that only the cobbler who is not a poet can provide workmanlike shoes.[1]

The persona is a collective phenomenon, a facet of the personality that might equally well belong to somebody else, but it is often mistaken for individuality. The actor or artist with long hair and casual clothes is looked on as someone unique – a personality – while often in fact he has simply adopted the dress and habits of all the other artists of his group. The friendliness and hospitality of Mrs So-and-So, the vicar's wife, seem to spring from her boundless good nature, but in reality she adopted these ways when she married her husband believing that 'a vicar's wife should be the friend of all who need her'. To some extent, it is true, people choose the roles for which they feel best fitted, and to this degree the persona is individual, but it is never the whole man or woman. Human nature is not consistent, yet in filling a role it must appear so, and is therefore inevitably falsified.

1. *Two Essays on Analytical Psychology*, p. 191.

The persona, however, is a necessity; through it we relate to our world. It simplifies our contacts by indicating what we may expect from other people, and on the whole makes them pleasanter, as good clothes improve ugly bodies.

People who neglect the development of a persona tend to be gauche, to offend others, and to have difficulty in establishing themselves in the world. There is always the danger, however, of identifying oneself with the role one fills, a danger that is not obvious when the role is a good one and fits the person well. Yet we often say with some concern 'he plays a part' or 'she is not really like that at all', for we are at least partly aware of the danger of living in a way that is not true to our real natures. Perhaps some crisis will occur which calls for flexibility or a completely new way of reacting, or a human situation may be reached where the lack of a genuinely individual emotional response spells tragedy. Elizabeth Bowen describes such a situation in *The Death of the Heart*, where the adults in the story are so locked in their conventional roles that they fail completely to understand the needs of a sensitive adolescent girl. Another danger is that too rigid a persona means too complete a denial of the rest of the personality, and all those aspects which have been relegated to the personal or belong to the collective unconscious.

Jung calls that other side of ourselves, which is to be found in the personal unconscious, the *shadow*. The shadow is the inferior being in ourselves, the one who wants to do all the things that we do not allow ourselves to do, who is everything that we are not, the Mr Hyde to our Dr Jekyll. We have an inkling of this foreign personality when, after being possessed by an emotion or overcome with rage, we excuse ourselves by saying, 'I was not myself', or 'I really don't know what came over me'. What 'came over' was in fact the shadow, the primitive, uncontrolled, and animal part of ourselves. The shadow also personifies itself: when we particularly dislike someone, especially if it is an unreasonable dislike, we should suspect that we are actually disliking a quality of our own which we find in the other person.

49

I do not love thee, Dr Fell.
The reason why I cannot tell.
But this alone I know full well,
I do not love thee, Dr Fell.

The shadow appears in dreams, personified as an inferior or very primitive person, someone with unpleasant qualities or someone we dislike.

The shadow is the personal unconscious; it is all those uncivilized desires and emotions that are incompatible with social standards and our ideal personality, all that we are ashamed of, all that we do not want to know about ourselves. It follows that the narrower and more restrictive the society in which we live the larger will be our shadow.

The shadow, since it is unconscious, cannot be touched by ordinary methods of education; it has remained much the same since infancy, when our actions were purely impulsive. It has probably remained much the same since man first walked the earth, for the shadow is the natural, i.e. the instinctive man.

The shadow is also something more than the personal unconscious – it is personal in so far as our own weaknesses and failings are concerned, but since it is common to humanity it can also be said to be a collective phenomenon. The collective aspect of the shadow is expressed as a devil, a witch, or something similar.

In choosing the word shadow to describe these aspects of the unconscious, Jung has more in mind than merely to suggest something dark and vague in outline. There is, as he points out, no shadow without the sun, and no shadow (in the sense of the personal unconscious) without the light of consciousness. It is in fact in the nature of things that there should be light and dark, sun and shade. The shadow is unavoidable and man is incomplete without it. Superstition holds that the man without a shadow (using the word in its ordinary sense) is the devil himself, while we ourselves are cautious with someone who seems 'too good to be true', as if we recognized instinctively that human nature needs the leaven of a little wickedness.

Jung, as a physician to whom people come in distress, has found it as useless to deny the shadow as to try to repress it completely. Man has, in his view, to find some way of living with his dark side; in fact his mental and physical health often depend on this. To accept the shadow involves considerable moral effort and often the giving up of cherished ideals, but only because the ideals were raised too high or based upon an illusion. Trying to live as better and nobler people than we are involves us in endless hypocrisy and deceit, and imposes such a strain on us that we often collapse and become worse than we need have been. The irritability and lack of tolerance of the over-virtuous are well known; the sexual life of the very respectable citizen is sometimes startling, as the daily papers show, and crime appears in most unexpected quarters; these are all manifestations of the shadow. It certainly takes moral courage to realize that these aspects of human nature may be, and probably are, lurking within ourselves, but there is comfort in the fact that once a thing is faced and known, there is at least some possibility of changing it, whereas in the unconscious nothing changes. A man who is unconsciously hating his wife so much that he wants to kill her, may actually do so in a fit of rage – such situations are not unknown; but if he had previously recognized his violent feelings he would have had the opportunity either to wrestle with them or to try to change the situation which provoked them.

While some repression is a necessity of social life, the danger of repressing the shadow is that in the unconscious it seems to acquire strength and grow in vigour, so that when the moment comes (as usually happens) when it must appear, it is more dangerous and more likely to overwhelm the rest of the personality, which otherwise could have acted as a wholesome check. This is particularly true of those collective aspects of the shadow which are displayed when a mob riots and apparently harmless people behave in the most appallingly savage and destructive manner.

'The shadow', says Jung, 'is a moral problem which challenges the whole ego personality'; it is moreover a social.

problem of immense importance which should not be under-estimated. No one is able to realize the shadow without con-siderable moral resolution, and some reorientation of his standards and ideas. Jung hints that no redemption is pos-sible without tolerance and love – attitudes that have proved fruitful in dealing with the social renegade, but that we do not usually think of applying in any constructive way to our-selves.

Having to some extent described the realm of the shadow, we can now pass deeper into the unconscious – in fact into the collective unconscious – but before going farther it is necessary to make a distinction between men on the one hand and women on the other. So far the term 'man' has been used for convenience in describing both man and woman, for each sex has equally a persona and a shadow, the only difference being that a man's shadow is personified by an-other man, a woman's shadow by another woman. It has already been said that the unconscious complements the conscious standpoint; to carry this farther, the unconscious of a man contains a complementary feminine element, that of a woman a male element. These Jung calls respectively the *anima* and the *animus*. It may seem paradoxical to suggest man is not wholly man nor woman wholly woman, yet it is a fairly common experience to find feminine and masculine traits in one person. The most masculine of men will often show surprising gentleness with children, or with anyone weak or ill; strong men give way to uncontrolled emotion in private, and can be both sentimental and irrational; brave men are sometimes terrified by quite harmless situations, and some men have surprising intuition or a gift for sensing other people's feelings. All these are supposedly feminine traits, as well as more obvious 'effeminacy' in a man. This latent femininity in a man is, however, only one aspect of his feminine soul, his anima. 'A collective image of woman exists in a man's unconscious,' says Jung, 'with the help of which he apprehends the nature of woman.'[1]

1. *Two Essays on Analytical Psychology*, p. 188.

But it is only woman as a general phenomenon that man apprehends in this way, for the image is an archetype, a representation of the age-old experience of man with woman, and though many women will conform, at least outwardly, to this image, it in no way represents the real character of an individual woman.

The image only becomes conscious and tangible through the actual contacts with woman that a man makes during the course of his life. The first and most important experience of a woman comes to him through his mother, and is most powerful in shaping and influencing him: there are men who never succeed in freeing themselves from her fascinating power. But the child's experience has a marked subjective character; it is not only how the mother behaves, but how he *feels* she behaves that is significant. The image of his mother that occurs in each child is not an accurate picture of her, but is formed and coloured by the innate capacity to produce an image of woman – the anima.

Later the image is projected on to the various women who attract a man in his lifetime. Naturally this leads to endless misunderstanding, for most men are unaware that they are projecting their own inner picture of woman on to someone very different; most inexplicable love affairs and disastrous marriages arise in this way. Unfortunately the projection is not something that can be controlled in a rational manner; a man does not make projections, they happen to him. 'Every mother and every beloved is forced to become the carrier and embodiment of this omnipresent and ageless image, which corresponds to the deepest reality in a man.'[1]

This image of a woman, because it is an archetype of the collective unconscious, has attributes that appear and reappear through the ages, whenever men are describing the women who are significant to them. In different eras the image may be slightly changed or modified, but some characteristics seem to remain almost constant; the anima has a

1. *Aion*, p. 13.

53

timeless quality – she often looks young, though there is always the suggestion of years of experience behind her. She is wise, but not formidably so; it is rather that 'something strangely meaningful clings to her, a secret knowledge or hidden wisdom'.[1] She is often connected with the earth, or with water, and she may be endowed with great power. She is also two-sided or has two aspects, a light and a dark, corresponding to the different qualities and types of women; on the one hand the pure, the good, the noble goddess-like figure, on the other the prostitute, the seductress, or the witch. It is when a man has repressed his feminine nature, when he under-values feminine qualities or treats women with contempt or neglect, that this dark aspect is most likely to present itself. Sometimes she appears to be faery-like or elfin in character and has the power to lure men away from their work or their homes, like the sirens of old or their more modern counterparts. She appears again and again in myth and literature as goddess and as 'femme fatale', 'The face that launched a thousand ships', 'La Belle Dame Sans Merci'; or in fairy-tales as the mermaid, water sprite, or nymph, who entices a man under the water where she lives so that he must love her for ever or be drowned.

The compelling power of the anima is due to her image being an archetype of the collective unconscious, which is projected on to any woman who offers the slightest hook on which her picture may be hung. Jung considers her to be the soul of man, not soul in the Christian sense, as the essence of the personality and with the attribute of immortality, but 'soul' as primitives conceive it to be – namely, a part of the personality. To avoid confusion, therefore, Jung uses the word anima instead of soul; psychologically it implies 'the recognition of the existence of a semiconscious psychic complex, having partial autonomy of function'.[2]

The anima carries spiritual values, and so her image is projected not only on to pagan goddesses, but on to

1. *The Archetypes and the Collective Unconscious*, p. 30, Collected Works, Vol. 9, Part 1.
2. *Two Essays*, p. 188.

the Virgin herself, but she is also near to nature and charged with emotion. She is 'chaotic urge to life',[1] she is a seductress, she is 'My Lady Soul',[2] and she is also the beckoning fair one luring men on to love and despair, to creative activity and to doom. She is in fact as thoroughly inconsistent as the woman in whose form she is always personified, and in describing her Jung usually chooses a dramatic and mythological approach as conveying 'the living processes of the psyche'[3] far more accurately than any abstract scientific formula.

The anima is expressed in a man's life not only in projection upon women and in creative activity, but in fantasies, moods, presentiments, and emotional outbursts. An old Chinese text says that when a man wakens in the morning heavy or in a bad mood, that is his feminine soul, his anima. She disturbs the attempt to concentrate by whispering absurd notions in his ear, spoils the day by creating the vague, unpleasant sensation that there is something physically wrong with him, or haunts his sleep with seductive visions; and a man possessed by his anima is a prey to uncontrollable emotion.

The *animus* in women is the counterpart of the anima in man. He seems to be (like the anima) derived from three roots: the collective image of man which a woman inherits; her own experience of masculinity coming through the contacts she makes with men in her life; and the latent masculine principle in herself.

The masculine principle – that is, the masculine element in women – found very positive expression in women's activities during the war years, when it was made clear that they could fill adequately most positions previously reserved for men. But only an abnormal situation brings out such manifestations; there is a contemporary movement towards a wider range of activity for women, but generally this activity is better expressed in a domestic *milieu,* or in one that bears some relationship to it, e.g. teaching, nursing, social

1. *The Archetypes and the Collective Unconscious*, p. 30.
2. Spitteler – quoted in *Aion*, p. 13.
3. *Ibid.*

work, &c. 'Personal relations are as a rule more important and interesting to her than objective facts and their interconnexions. The wide fields of commerce, politics, technology, and science, the whole realm of the applied masculine mind, she relegates to the penumbra of consciousness; while on the other hand, she develops a minute consciousness of personal relationships, the infinite nuances of which usually escape the man entirely.'[1]

In other words, it is usually (though not always) the case that a woman's thinking and a man's feeling and emotion belong to the realm of the unconscious. The anima produces *moods*, the animus produces *opinions*, resting on unconscious assumptions instead of really conscious and directed thought.

As the mother is the first carrier of the anima image for the boy, so the father embodies the animus image for the girl, and this combination seems to exercise a profound and lasting fascination over her mind, so that instead of thinking and acting for herself she continually quotes father and does things in father's way, even late into life.

In the course of normal development the animus becomes projected on to many male figures, and when this projection has been made, a woman takes for granted that a man is as she sees him (i.e. in the guise of the animus), and it is almost impossible for her to accept him as he really is. This attitude can be very troublesome in personal relationships, which only go smoothly so long as the man conforms to the assumptions that the woman is making about him. The animus can be personified as any male figure, from the most primitive to the most spiritual, depending on the state of a woman's development. He can even appear in dreams as a boy, and is often heard simply as a voice.

Another peculiarity of the animus, as distinct from the anima, which is always seen as one woman, is its tendency to be expressed as a group of men.[2] To quote Jung:

1. *Two Essays on Analytical Psychology*, p. 205.
2. A particularly good example of this occurs in H. G. Wells's novel *Christina Alberta's Father*.

The animus is rather like an assembly of fathers or dignitaries of some kind who lay down incontestable, 'rational', *ex cathedra* judgements. On closer examination these exacting judgements turn out to be largely sayings and opinions scraped together more or less unconsciously from childhood on, and compressed into a canon of average truth, justice, and reasonableness, a compendium of preconceptions which, whenever a conscious and competent judgement is lacking (as not infrequently happens), instantly obliges with an opinion. Sometimes these opinions take the form of so-called sound common sense, sometimes they appear as principles which are like a travesty of education: 'People have always done it like this', or 'Everybody says it is like that'.[1]

This critical judgement is sometimes turned on the woman herself as an over-active conscience, giving her feelings of inferiority and stifling initiative. At other times it is directed on the people round her in a thoroughly destructive and indiscriminating fashion. She will then criticize her neighbours, tear strangers' characters to pieces without a shred of real evidence, or make disparaging remarks to her family or the people with whom she works on the grounds that 'it is good for them'. 'I believe in calling a spade a spade' or 'I don't believe in spoiling them' are typical animus statements. An intelligent and educated woman is just as much a victim of this animus power as her less-educated sister. The latter will quote the daily paper or some vague body called 'They' to support her convictions – 'They say it's so' or 'I saw it in the paper' – while the former will rely on some authoritative body; the university, the Church, the State, or perhaps some book or historical document. In either case if her opinion is questioned she will become argumentative and dogmatic. This side of a woman craves power, and however gentle and adaptable she may be in her everyday life, she becomes tyrannical and aggressive once her animus side is aroused, and is quite blind to any reason. Because of this animus activity it is really difficult for a woman to think in an unprejudiced way. She needs to be always on her guard against the inner voice which is continually telling her that

1. *Two Essays*, p. 206.

'it should be this way' or 'they ought to do that', and which makes it impossible for her to see things as they really are.

The animus has a positive function, however; there are times when a woman needs the courage and aggressiveness he represents, and he is useful if she can prevent him running away with her; the opinions produced by him are too generalized, and therefore inapplicable to any particular situation, but if a woman really attempts to understand them critically she may find something of value in them. The animus can in fact stir her to search for knowledge and truth, and lead her into purposeful activity, if she can learn to know him and delineate his sphere of activity.

Both the animus and the anima are mediators between the conscious and the unconscious mind, and when they become personified in fantasies, dreams, or visions they present an opportunity to understand something of what has hitherto been unconscious. Jung, as has already been said, takes dreams seriously. They are 'the voice of nature', and not only a voice, for they also have an effect on us. The most curious and apparently meaningless dreams can usually be understood if given the right kind of thought and consideration, while some present such a clear picture that there is little difficulty in grasping something of their meaning if one is prepared to try. If one studies visionary or dream figures closely and notes any correspondence with people already known, or with figures of myth and poetry, or characters from books or plays, one may gather some idea of the significance of the dream figure for oneself, and a hint of its unconscious influence.[1]

This is a tremendous gain, for the personality becomes freer and less subject to irrational and unseen influences. Moreover, relationships with other people become easier, for they can be seen as they are, instead of figures on whom we have draped our fancies and endowed with every possible and impossible characteristic, i.e. on whom we have projected ourselves.

1. The question of the understanding and interpretation of dreams is expanded in Chapter 6.

The influence of the anima and animus is far more difficult to grasp than that of the persona or the shadow. Most
people know someone who is so completely 'persona' that
they cannot fail to see its effects, and the shadow is sufficiently obtrusive to be recognized when pointed out. The
anima and animus are, however, elusive, and only a certain
number of people can understand what is meant by them.
Neither can they be completely integrated into consciousness; something of them remains always shrouded in mystery
in the dark realm of the collective unconscious. A man, for
instance, by accepting and learning to know his anima, may
become more receptive, or he may develop his intuition or
his feeling, but he cannot possess himself of those qualities
which are projected on to goddesses or on to the Virgin.
They may be present in him as mercy, benevolence, healing,
creativeness, and so on; but they are not really subject to his
will – they work sometimes even in spite of it – and they
cannot be called up just when he desires. The same is
true of women who can acquire the enterprise or develop
the thinking which belongs to them in a personal sense,
but can never possess as their own that aspect of the masculine spirit which belongs to the collective unconscious
and manifests itself as something beyond the purely personal.

Anyone, however, who has learnt to know something of
the anima or animus will have gained both knowledge of
him or herself, and of the forces which activate other human
beings; he or she will have plumbed something of the depths
of the collective unconscious, but will be far from having ex-
hausted this great ocean, which is, so far as we know, limit-
less. There is no question of draining the unconscious, or of
clearing out its contents. The archetypes which may emerge
from it are innumerable, and all one can do is to delineate
and become familiar as far as is possible with those which
seem to have the greatest significance and most powerful influence on us.

After the anima and animus the two archetypes which are
likely to become influential in a person's life are those of the

old wise man and the great mother. Jung sometimes calls the old wise man the archetype of meaning, but since he appears in various other forms – for instance as a king or hero, medicine man, or saviour – one must clearly take the word 'meaning' in its widest sense.

This archetype represents a serious danger to personality, for when it is awakened a man may easily come to believe that he really possesses the 'mana', the seemingly magical power and wisdom that it holds. It is as if the fascination of the anima had been transferred to this figure, and the one possessed by it feels himself endowed with great (perhaps esoteric) wisdom, prophetic powers, the gift of healing, and so on. Such a man may even gather a following, for in extending his awareness of the unconscious up to this point he has in fact gone farther than others; moreover, there is a compelling power in an archetype which people sense intuitively and cannot easily resist. They are fascinated by what he says, even though on reflection it often proves to be incomprehensible. But the power can be destructive and can compel a man to act beyond his strength and capacity; he does not really possess the wisdom, which is in fact a voice from the unconscious, and needs to be subjected to conscious criticism and understanding for its true value to become accessible. If a man believes he is voicing his own thoughts and expressing his own powers, when really some idea is emerging from the unconscious, he is in danger of possession and of megalomania. (The lunatic who thinks that he is king or is in communication with the great ones of the earth is an extreme example of the same kind of thing.) If, however, the man can quietly 'listen' to the voice of the unconscious and understand that the power works through him – he is not in control – then he is on the way to a genuine development of personality.

The archetype of the great mother acts in a parallel way on a woman. Anyone possessed by this figure comes to believe herself endowed with an infinite capacity for loving and understanding, helping and protecting, and will wear herself out in the service of others. She can, however, also be most destructive, insisting (though not necessarily openly) that all who come within her circle of influence are 'her children', and therefore helpless or dependent on her in some degree. This subtle tyranny, if carried to extremes, can demoralize and destroy the personality of others.

Jung calls possession by these archetypes 'inflation', indicating that the person so possessed has been, as it were, blown up by something too big for himself, something that is not really personal at all, but collective. In H. G. Wells's *Christina Alberta's Father* there's a good example of such an inflation, though it has not come about through an extension of consciousness and the assimilation of the anima, but through what Jung aptly terms 'an invasion from the collective unconscious': 'Mr Preemby, a midget personality, discovers that he is really a reincarnation of Sargon, King of Kings. Happily, the genius of the author rescues poor old Sargon from pathological absurdity, and even gives the reader a chance to appreciate the tragic and eternal meaning in this lamentable affray. Mr Preemby, a complete nonentity, recognizes himself as the point of intersection of all ages past and future. This knowledge is not too dearly bought at the cost of a little madness, provided that Preemby is not in the end devoured by that monster of a primordial image – which is in fact what nearly happens to him.'[1]

The feeling of godlikeness, of being a superman, which comes through inflation is an illusion. We may for a brief time possess phenomenal courage, or be infinitely wise or forgiving, but this is something 'beyond ourselves', and something that we cannot muster at will. We do not really understand the forces that move human beings in this way, and an attitude of humility in the face of them is absolutely necessary. But if the ego can relinquish some of the belief in its own omnipotence, a position can be found somewhere between that of consciousness with its hardly-won values, and unconsciousness with its vitality and power, and a new centre of personality can emerge, differing in its

1. *Two Essays*, p. 179.

nature from the ego-centre. Jung calls this new centre of personality '*the self*'.[1]

The ego, he says, can only be regarded as the centre of the conscious, and if it tries to add unconscious contents to itself (i.e. collective contents, not the personal unconscious or shadow which does belong to the ego) it is in danger of destruction, like an overloaded vessel which sinks under the strain. The self, however, can include both the conscious and the unconscious. It appears to act as something like a magnet to the disparate elements of the personality and the processes of the unconscious, and is the centre of this totality as the ego is the centre of consciousness, for it is the function which unites all the opposing elements in man and woman, consciousness and unconsciousness, good and bad, male and female, &c., and in so doing transmutes them. To reach it necessitates acceptance of what is inferior in one's nature, as well as what is irrational and chaotic.

This state cannot be reached by a mature person without considerable struggle; it implies suffering, for the Western mind, unlike the Eastern, does not easily tolerate paradoxes. For the Hindu everything, *highest* and *lowest*, is in the (transcendental) subject ... the self'.[2]

In Chinese thought the concept of Tao is also all-inclusive, and the development of the Golden Flower, or Immortal Spirit body (the highest aim of Chinese Yoga), depends on the equal interplay of both the light forces (*Yang*) and the dark forces (*Yin*).[3]

It was contact with the Eastern mind that illuminated for Jung many of the secrets of the unconscious and led him to formulate in *The Secret of the Golden Flower* the concept of the self. But he does not suggest that we should imitate the East in any way – to do so would be to become ridiculous,

---

1. The term 'self' is not used by Jung as in everyday speech, but in the Eastern manner, where as Atman, Purusha, Brahman, it has been a familiar philosophical concept from time immemorial. In Hindu thought the self is the supreme principle, the supreme oneness of being.

2. *Psychology and Alchemy*, p. 8.

3. Cf. *The Secret of the Golden Flower*, Wilhelm and Jung, pp. 12–13.

and like trying to wear every day a gorgeous fancy dress. 'That painstakingly forged instrument, the will'; and the vast body of knowledge laboriously acquired by the physicist, the chemist, the natural scientist, and so on, are not to be lightly thrown overboard.

Science is the best tool of the Western mind and with it more doors can be opened than with bare hands. Thus it ... only clouds our insight when it lays claim to being the one and only way of comprehending. But it is the East that has taught us another, wider, more profound and a higher understanding, that is, understanding through life. ... When faced with the problem of grasping the ideas of the East, the usual mistake of this Western man is ... to turn his back on science, and, getting a whiff of Eastern ecstatics, to take over their Yoga practices quite literally, only to become a pitiable imitator. (Theosophy is our best example of this mistake.)[1]

Jung makes it clear that his concept of the self is not that of a kind of universal consciousness, which is really only another name for the unconscious. It consists rather in the awareness on the one hand of our unique natures, and on the other of our intimate relationship with all life, not only human, but animal and plant, and even that of inorganic matter and the cosmos itself. It brings a feeling of 'oneness', and of reconciliation with life, which can now be accepted as it is, not as it ought to be.

It is as if the leadership of the affairs of life had gone over to an invisible centre ... [and there is a] release from compulsion and impossible responsibility which are the inevitable results of *participation mystique*.[2]

Jung watched the growth of this new centre of personality in scores of his patients before attempting to formulate it in this way. It should not be thought, however, that all who choose to submit to the process of analysis have this experience or reach this state of development. For many people it is enough to free themselves from their unconscious childish dependence, to be relieved of a distressing symptom through

1. *The Secret of the Golden Flower*, Wilhelm and Jung, pp. 78, 79.
2. *The Secret of the Golden Flower*, pp. 132–3.

the recognition of its cause, or to have worked out a new and more satisfactory adaptation to life. But there are some who are forced to take full account of the unconscious, who must find a way to know and accept its life side by side with that of consciousness, who must in fact integrate it in such a way that their personality is whole. For, paradoxically, the self is not only the centre, but represents the whole man; making a unity out of the contradictions of his nature, all that is felt to be good, and all that is felt to be bad; maleness and femaleness, the four functions of thinking, feeling, sensation, and intuition: the conscious and the unconscious.

'The self,' says Jung, 'is not only the centre, but also the circumference that encloses consciousness and the unconscious; it is the centre of this totality, as the ego is the centre of consciousness.'[1]

The experience of the self is archetypal, and it is portrayed in dreams and visions by many and varied images, all of which may be called archetypes of the self. To those unfamiliar with the language of dreams this wide variety of images may seem confusing, but one must remember that the unconscious is never precise in the way that consciousness needs to be.

If [it speaks] of the sun and identifies it with the lion, the king, the hoard of gold guarded by the dragon, or the power that makes for the life and health of man, it is neither the one thing nor the other, but the unknown third thing that finds more or less adequate expression in all these similes; yet – to the perpetual vexation of the intellect – remains unknown and not to be fitted into a formula.[2]

A child is a frequent symbol of the self, sometimes a divine or magical child, sometimes an ordinary figure, or even a ragamuffin. The endless preoccupation of myth and folklore with the child motive, and the high place it occupies in many religions, and especially in Christianity, throw considerable light on the meaning of the child as a symbol of the self. At the other extreme come the figures of Christ and of Buddha,

1. *The Integration of the Personality*, p. 96, 'Dream Symbols of the Process of Individuation'.
2. 'The Psychology of the Child Archetype', p. 157, Collected Works, Vol. 9, Part 1.

which in Jung's view are the most highly differentiated expressions of the archetype of the self yet reached by mankind.[1]

The self can also develop in dreams from an animal, or an egg; it is found expressed as a hermaphroditic figure (an obvious symbol of completeness) or again as 'the treasure hard to attain'. In this case it is often a jewel (especially a diamond or pearl), a flower, a golden egg or ball, or a chalice. Geometric figures such as the circle, the wheel, and the square, and anything fourfold, from the cross with equal arms to the homely symbol of four nuts arranged upon a plate, also appear frequently as symbols of the self.

These concentrically arranged figures are often known as 'mandalas'. Mandala is a Sanskrit word meaning magic circle, and its symbolism includes all concentrically arranged figures, all radial or spherical arrangements, and all circles or squares with a central point. It is one of the oldest religious symbols (the earliest known form being the sun wheel), and is found throughout the world. In the East the mandala (whose form is fixed by tradition) is used ritualistically in Lamaistic and Tantric Yoga as an aid to contemplation. There are Christian mandalas, dating from the early Middle Ages, showing Christ in the centre with the four evangelists and their symbols at the cardinal points. Historically, the mandala served as a symbol representing the nature of the deity, both in order to clarify it philosophically, and for the purpose of adoration.

Jung found the mandala symbolism occurring spontaneously in the dreams and visions of many of his patients.[2] Its

---

1. *Psychology and Alchemy*, par. 22. 'We can see this from the scope and substance of all the pronouncements that have been made about Christ; they agree with the psychological phenomenology of the self in unusually high degree, although they do not include all the aspects of this archetype.' It is not to be thought that this statement implies anything other than a psychological fact, namely that the unconscious produces images of a Christlike and a Buddha-like character. This point will be discussed further in the chapter on Psychology and Religion.

2. *The Secret of the Golden Flower*, Wilhelm and Jung. A series of 400 dreams in which the mandala symbolism occurs is studied in *The Integration of the Personality* and in *Psychology and Alchemy*.

appearance was incomprehensible to them, but it was usually accompanied by a strong feeling of harmony or of peace. The mandala was sometimes drawn or painted, in which case it frequently took an abstract geometric form, and at other times seen as a vision (either waking or in a dream) or danced. If dancing a mandala strikes the reader as strange, he need only remember the many examples of ritual dances, or even of folk-dances, where there is a circling round a central point, a withdrawal to the four corners, and an advance to the centre. Mandala visions may occur as the outcome of what Jung calls 'active imagination' which is a technique of 'intense concentration on the background of consciousness, that is perfected only after long practice'.[1] Here is an example from a long sequence given by a woman patient:

I climbed the mountain and came to a place where I saw seven red stones in front of me, seven on either side, and seven behind me. I stood in the middle of this quadrangle. The stones were flat like steps. I tried to lift the four stones nearest me. In doing so I discovered that these stones were the pedestals of four statues of gods buried upside down in the earth. I dug them up and arranged them about me so that I was standing in the middle of them. Suddenly they leaned towards one another, until their heads touched, forming something like a tent over me. I myself fell to the ground and said 'Fall upon me if you must; I am tired'. Then I saw that beyond, encircling the four gods, a ring of flame had formed. After a time I got up from the ground and overthrew the statues of the gods. Where they fell, four trees shot up. At that blue flames leapt up from the ring of fire and began to burn the foliage of the trees. Seeing this I said: 'This must stop. I must go into the fire myself so that the leaves shall not be burned.' Then I stepped into the fire. The trees vanished and the fiery ring drew together to one immense blue flame that carried me up from the earth.[2]

It is not possible to go fully into the meaning of this vision, but at least the reader will recognize the idea of a mid-point which is reached with effort and by accepting danger, and notice that the quadrangle and the circle are important features.

1. *Two Essays on Analytical Psychology*, p. 220.
2. *Ibid.*

A more abstract vision is that of the world clock, which was recorded by a young intellectual, who had come to Jung with a severe neurosis. An interesting point is that this young man was only seen by Jung for a short interview, after which he recorded his dreams and visual experiences for five months with a pupil – a woman doctor who was then a beginner – and then continued his observations alone for another three months. The possibility of Jung's influence on the material he produced was thus reduced to a minimum.

The vision was as follows:

There is a vertical and a horizontal circle, having a common centre. It is supported by the black bird. The vertical circle is a blue disk with a white border, divided into 4 × 8 equalling 32 partitions. A hand is rotating upon it. The horizontal circle consists of four colours. On it stand four little men with pendulums, and round about it is laid the [golden] ring.[1]

This vision produced a feeling of sublime harmony in the patient, and is of such interest that it has been the subject of much research on Jung's part.[2]

But mandala symbolism may also be simpler and less dramatic than these two examples: a dream of a square with a fountain in the centre and people walking round the fountain, or of a square garden with a circular flower-bed in the middle, or something equally everyday, can have a like significance, though the impact it makes on the dreamer may not be so marked.

Jung found that the experience which was ultimately formulated in the mandala pattern was typical of people who were no longer able to project the divine image – i.e. to find God somewhere outside themselves – and so were in danger of inflation. The round or square enclosures seemed to act like magically protective walls, preventing an outburst and a disintegration, and protecting an inward purpose. There was a similarity in them to the sacred places that in ancient times were often made to protect the God, but the significant fact

1. *Psychology and Religion*, p. 66.
2. Recorded in *Psychology and Religion*, *Psychology and Alchemy*, and *The Integration of the Personality*.

about a modern mandala is that it rarely if ever contains a god in the centre, but instead a variety of symbols, or even a human being. A modern mandala is therefore 'an involuntary confession of a peculiar mental condition. There is no deity in the mandala, nor is there any submission or reconciliation to a deity. The place of the deity seems to be taken by the wholeness of man.'[1]

1. *Psychology and Religion*, p. 82.

CHAPTER 4

Religion and the Individuation Process

THE study of the archetypes of the collective unconscious has led Jung to some interesting conclusions, one of the most important of which is that man possesses what he describes as 'a natural religious function', and that his psychic health and stability depend on the proper expression of this, just as much as on the expression of the instincts. This is in direct contrast to those who view religion as an illusion, an escape from reality, or a childish weakness. So widespread has this attitude become, even if not consciously realized, that we have almost lost sight of the important part that religion has played in our history, the intensity of emotion it aroused, and the tremendous energy it canalized into the arts, into the creation of fine buildings, into learning, teaching, and caring for the weak, the sick, and the poor. The lovely cathedrals and the large churches which adorn even tiny villages are standing evidence of its past influences, just as priests' hiding-holes and Huguenot surnames are reminders of more sinister aspects of the religious spirit, its fanaticism and its cruel energy in persecuting all those who did not see eye to eye with it.

We think ourselves more rational to-day, and more tolerant, or rather we did so until those modern versions of religious persecution arose, which were disguised as political necessities. There was scarcely any hiding the fact that, for instance, in Germany 'a religious spirit' expressed almost openly as the worship of Wotan, with all its pagan accompaniments, supplied some of the dynamic energy that permeated the Nazi movement,[1] just as 'a religious spirit' also

1. The Nazi German youth movement celebrated the solstice and sacrificed sheep. An evangelical clergyman, dressed in S.A. uniform and top boots, in a funeral address, sped the deceased on his journey to Hades,

opposed this movement, but there is a persistent tendency in us to dissociate ourselves from such things. We are sure they could not happen to us. Jung reminds us, however, that these movements are manifestations of the collective unconscious which is common to all mankind. Moreover, 'the archetypes of the collective unconscious can be shown empirically to be the equivalents of religious dogmas'[1] and they correspond to all the known religious ideas. (This must not be taken to mean that the unconscious actually produces religious dogmas – these are the product of conscious thought working on and refining the raw material of the unconscious.)

Through the study of the archetypes of the collective unconscious we find that man possesses 'a religious function' and that this influences him in its way as powerfully as do the instincts of sexuality and aggression. Primitive man is as occupied with the expression of this function – the forming of symbols and the building up of a religion – as he is with tilling the earth, hunting, fishing, and the fulfilment of his other basic needs; and in spite of the modern attitude of denigration, men and women are just as naturally religious as ever they were. Much, however, of the energy that formerly flowed into ritual and religious observance now finds expression in political creeds, or is frittered away in peculiar cults, or attached to something extraneous like the pursuit of knowledge. 'A scientist has no creed', says William James, 'but his temper is devout', while Julian Huxley suggests in all seriousness that we should have a religion based on evolution:[2]

... evolutionary humanism, it seems to me, is capable of becoming the germ of a new religion, not necessarily supplanting existing religions but supplementing them. It remains to see how this germ

---

and directed him to Valhalla, the home of Siegfried and Baldur, the heroes. *Essays on Contemporary Events*, 'Wotan'.

1. *Psychology and Alchemy*, p. 17.

2. Quoted from a series of radio talks entitled 'The Process of Evolution' reproduced in the *Listener*, 22 November 1951.

could be developed – to work out its intellectual framework, to see how its ideas could be made inspiring, to ensure their wide diffusion. Above all, it would be necessary to justify ideas by facts to find the areas of frustration and point out where they were being reduced; to show how research into human possibilities was providing new incentives for their realization, as well as demonstrating the means for realizing them.

Such a religion, for all its nobility of purpose, would fail to fill the deepest human need – that is, to relate the inner and outer man in equal degree. It is an essential feature of religion to give conscious expression to the archetypes; no completely rational system can succeed in this, and religious 'truths' are therefore always paradoxical. If religion tries to avoid paradox it merely weakens itself.

Jung defines religion as 'a peculiar attitude of mind which could be formulated in accordance with the original use of the word "religio", which means a careful consideration and observation of certain dynamic factors, that are conceived as "powers"; spirits, demons, gods, laws, ideals, or whatever name man has given to such factors in his world as he has found powerful, dangerous, or helpful enough to be taken into careful consideration, or grand, beautiful, and meaningful enough to be devoutly worshipped and loved'.[1]

The operative word in this definition is 'dynamic'; it is the dynamism of the religious function that makes it both futile and dangerous to try to explain it away. This dynamism was expressed in the past in the great proselytizing movements, in crusades, religious wars, and persecutions, in heresy hunts and witch hunts, and in the creative efforts which caused men to build vast tombs and places of worship filled with every kind of treasure. To-day much of this energy finds its expression in the various 'isms' – Communism, Nazism, Fascism, &c. – and rouses men to dangerous ardour, or expends itself in cults which have borrowed indiscriminately from the East. Superstition is rife in spite of general education, and persecution in varying degrees of cruelty and intolerance is all too common.

1. *Psychology and Religion*, p. 8.

What organized religion has always tried to do, with varying success, has been to provide satisfying forms for those deep human needs which now find such dangerous or banal expression, and to express 'the living process of the unconscious in the form of the drama of repentance, sacrifice and redemption'.[1] Dogma, creed, and ritual are crystallized forms of *original religious experience*, worked over and refined, sometimes for centuries, until they reach the forms in which we know them. In this way channels are made which control the unruly and arbitrary 'supernatural' influences. A living church protects men from the full force of an experience which can be devastating; instead of being gripped by the collective unconscious, they can participate in a ritual which expresses it sufficiently to 'purge' by its reflection.

What this original experience may mean is vividly recorded for us in the Bible, in the stories of the prophets and the account, for instance, of the conversion of Saul. After Saul had seen the bright light that shone from heaven and heard a voice saying unto him 'Saul, Saul, why persecutest thou me?' he became blind for three days and could neither eat nor drink, and from his recovery his whole life was changed.

Jung illustrates the effort of 'immediate' religious experience by the story of the Swiss mystic and hermit, 'the blessed brother Nicholas von der Flüe'. Brother Nicholas had a 'vision of threefoldness', so terrible in its nature that his whole face was changed and his appearance from then on terrified people. He himself was so preoccupied by the vision that he made wide researches into its nature and even painted it on the wall of his cell. A contemporary picture in the parish church of Sachseln shows us that this painting was a mandala, divided into six, with the crowned countenance of God in the centre. This is clearly not the original terrifying vision, but a development from it. Brother Nicholas, as Jung says, in struggling to get his original experience into tangible form,

[was] inevitably led ... to the conclusion that he must have gazed

1. *Psychology and Religion*, p. 46.

upon the Holy Trinity itself – the *summum bonum*, eternal love. This is borne out by the 'expurgated' version now in Sachseln. ... This vision, undoubtedly fearful and highly perturbing, ... naturally needed a long labour of assimilation in order to fit it into the total structure of the psyche and thus restore the disturbed psychic balance. Brother Klaus came to terms with his experience on the basis of dogma, then firm as a rock; and the dogma proved its powers of assimilation by turning something horribly alive into the beautiful abstraction of the Trinity idea.[1]

The experience of the God-image or archetype of the self is at once the most vital and the most overwhelming that can happen to man, and without some anchor he may be swept away. The dogma provided this anchor for Brother Nicholas. Furthermore the expression of the archetype depends upon the receiving consciousness; it can be infinitely developed and refined, as it has been in the highest religions of the world, or it can be relatively simple and archaic, as in the more primitive cults.

It can also destroy a weak consciousness altogether, so that the result is not a religious development, but insanity, or a pathological manifestation, as in the woman who believes she is to repeat the miracle of the virgin birth, or the decrepit old man who asks everyone he meets whether they are 'saved'.

To suggest that there are psychic factors which correspond to the divine figures, and that there can even be a like element in the absurdities of the insane and the experiences of the mystic, might be (and often is) taken as a devaluation of the latter, and even 'smacks of blasphemy', yet we are prepared to accept that 'genius is next to madness'. Jung, however, far from belittling religious experience, not only demonstrates the existence of the religious function in individuals and opens a way to its comprehension 'by reason as well as feeling', but stresses that 'it is the prime task of all education (of adults) to convey the archetype of the God-image, or its emanations and effects, to the conscious mind'.[2]

1. *The Archetypes and the Collective Unconscious*, p. 9.
2. *Psychology and Alchemy*, p. 12.

73

This is what Christian education has tried to do, but 'the Western attitude, with its emphasis on the object, tends to fix the ideal – Christ – in its outward aspect and thus to rob it of its mysterious relation to the inner man'.[1]

It is this attitude which, in projecting everything good on to a remote figure of God, and everything bad on to an even more remote figure of the Devil, robs the psyche of its value and meaning and leads on the one hand to an over-valuation of consciousness and on the other to the deification of abstractions like the State. In addition, creed and ritual have become so elaborated and refined that they no longer express the psychic state of the ordinary man, and religion has congealed into externals and formalities.

Man needs to experience the god-image within himself and to feel its correspondence with the forms that his religion gives to it. If this does not happen there is a split in his nature; he may be outwardly civilized, but inwardly he is a barbarian ruled by an archaic god.

Not the individual alone but the sum total of individual lives in a people proves the truth of this contention. The great events of our world as planned and executed by man do not breathe the spirit of Christianity, but rather of unadorned paganism. These things originate in a psychic condition that has remained archaic and has not been even remotely touched by Christianity. The Church assumes, not altogether without reason, that the fact of *semel credidisse* (having once believed) leaves certain traces behind it; but of these traces nothing is to be seen in the march of events. Christian civilization has proved hollow to a terrifying degree: it is all veneer, but the inner man has remained untouched and therefore unchanged. His soul is out of key with his external beliefs; in his soul the Christian has not kept pace with external developments. Yes, everything is to be found outside – in image and in word, in Church and Bible – but never inside. Inside reign the archaic gods, supreme as of old; that is to say the inner correspondence with the outer God-image is undeveloped for lack of psychological culture and has therefore got stuck in heathenism. Christian education has done all that is humanly possible, but it has not been enough. Too few people have experienced the divine image as the inner-

1. *Psychology and Alchemy*, p. 8.

74

most possession of their own souls. Christ only meets them from without, never from within the soul; that is why dark paganism still reigns there, a paganism which, now in a form so blatant that it can no longer be denied and now in all too threadbare disguise, is swamping the world of so-called Christian culture.[1]

This pagan unconscious, which has also influenced our literature and art, is clearly expressed in dreams long before it becomes apparent in action. A clergyman, for instance, in some doubt about his faith had the following dream:

> I come at night into my church. There the whole wall of the choir has fallen together. The altar and the ruins are grown over with vines that are full of grapes, and through the opening that has been made shines the moon.[2]

This dream is picturesque and symbolic and remembering the symbolical and analogical character of dream imagery it is not very difficult to grasp that the outward expression of faith – i.e. the Church – is collapsing, and that something 'natural' is creeping in. The vine was an early Christian symbol – 'I am the vine and ye are the branches'; it was also an important symbol of the orgiastic worship of the God Pan. The moon gives a romantic and slightly mysterious air to the whole picture; once it was regarded as a god or goddess and worshipped accordingly, and it is significant to remember this.

In these analogies we have a hint of what this dream meant to the dreamer; here is another which pictures even more clearly a state of mind that is out of harmony with a modern rational outlook – it was dreamt by a cultivated middle-aged woman:

> There was an enclosed but empty space. In the centre, on the ground, burnt a small fire with a plume of smoke rising from it. I was on my knees in front of the fire, and bowing my head I chanted rhythmically, 'God is in the smoke, God is in the smoke'.

There are also dreams which point in the opposite direc-

---

1. *Psychology and Alchemy*, pp. 11–12.
2. *The Integration of the Personality*, p. 150, cf. *Psychology and Alchemy*, par. 179, p. 135.

tion, and can demonstrate (if he will but take notice) to a confirmed agnostic that he is really a believer at heart, or lead a renegade back to the faith he has forsaken. Many a neurosis can be cured if the sufferer can find his way back to the Church where he belonged, or experience a conversion; but these solutions cannot be imposed, they must arise from the inner need of that particular person and his awareness and understanding of that need. If, however, the mental health of the individual and the progress of civilization depend to so large an extent on the suitable expression of the religious function, what solution is there for those who cannot return to any Church, or find in the 'Christian drama' no satisfactory expression of their needs?

Jung found the answer to this question gradually evolved itself during years of work with patients, and borrowed the word 'individuation' to describe it. There were, he found, a relatively large number of people who, while cured in the ordinary sense of the word, either persisted in continuing their analytical treatment, 'the dialectical discussion between the conscious mind and the unconscious',[1] or followed it on their own account away from the analyst. They were mature people, and were not 'hanging on' to their analyst from fear of life or because of that peculiar attachment which in psychological terms is called 'a transference';[2] it was rather that they were unconsciously and yet unswervingly seeking a goal, which eventually defined itself as the quest of wholeness – that mysterious entity 'the whole man' – and which necessitated the forging of a link between the conscious and the unconscious aspects of the psyche. The experience could also be formulated as the finding of the God within or the full experience of the archetype of the self.

This is a state which cannot be reached without suffering, and necessitates accepting freely many things which are shunned by the ordinary man or woman; nor is analysis the only way of reaching the goal, but it is one which fits the

1. *Psychology and Alchemy*, p. 4.
2. See chapter on Psychotherapy.

modern dilemma particularly well. This dilemma is summed up in the passage already quoted in Chapter 3:

There is no deity in the [modern] mandala, nor is there any submission or reconciliation to a deity. The place of the deity seems to be taken by the wholeness of man.[1]

The individuation process is one which develops gradually during a person's life, more noticeably in the second half of life, and though it was observed by Jung in 'patients', one must not think of it as either a neurotic or a pathological phenomenon.

To be whole means to become reconciled with those sides of personality which have not been taken into account; these are often but not always inferior, for there are people who do not live up to the possibilities inherent in themselves. No one who really seeks wholeness can develop his intellect at the price of repression of the unconscious, nor, on the other hand, can he live in a more or less unconscious state.

Conscious and unconscious do not make a whole when one of them is suppressed and injured by the other. If they must contend, let it at least be a fair fight with equal rights on both sides. Both are aspects of life. Consciousness should defend its reason and protect itself, and the chaotic life of the unconscious should be given the chance of having its way too – as much of it as we can stand. This means open conflict and open collaboration at once. That, evidently, is the way human life should be. It is the old game of hammer and anvil: between them the patient iron is forged into an indestructible whole, an 'individual'. This, roughly, is what I mean by the individuation process.[2]

The whole man is an individual, but he is not individualistic, which means being ego-centred, and is often used as an excuse to develop peculiarities at the expense of other people or to behave in an egotistical fashion. The individuated person, on the other hand, through his acceptance of the unconscious has, while remaining aware of his unique personality,

1. *Psychology and Religion*, p. 82.
2. *The Archetypes and the Collective Unconscious*, p. 288, 'Conscious, Unconscious, and Individuation'.

realized his brotherhood with all living things, even with inorganic matter and the cosmos itself.

No man is an Iland, intire of itselfe; every man is a peece of the Continent, a part of the maine; if a Clod bee washed away by the sea, Europe is the lesse, as well as if a Promontorie were, as well as if a Mannor of thy friends or thine own were; any man's death diminishes me, because I am involved in Mankind; and therefore never send to know for whom the bell tolls; it tolls for thee.[1]

Individuation is not usually an aim or an ideal for the very young, but rather for the mature person or for those who have been impelled by a serious illness, a neurosis, or some unusual experience to leave the ordinary safe paths and look for a new way of living. This not infrequently happens to middle-aged people, who having been successful in their chosen career, suddenly wake to a feeling of emptiness and lack of meaning in their lives. Such a case is described in detail by Jung in *The Integration of the Personality*.

Jung regards it as extremely important to differentiate between what he calls 'the stages of life'. The first half he compares to the morning, when the sun seems to rise above the horizon and climb slowly to the meridian, the second half to the afternoon, when the sun, completing the curve, sinks again and finally disappears. What is appropriate to the morning of life is not suitable for the afternoon. The young man needs to establish himself in the world, find a suitable wife, and build up a family, the young woman to marry, have children, and fulfil the social obligations of her position. Each needs to concentrate on one aspect of his or her personality: in the man's case the development of his intellect or his special skill, and in the woman's case the sacrifice of those gifts and qualities which would enable her to make her mark in the world are required. From both, usefulness, efficiency, and social adaptation are demanded, and their energies must be directed this way. Our society is based on scientific knowledge and technical skill, and in acquiring this men are inevitably forced to develop one-sidedly, sharpening

1. *Devotions upon Emergent Occasions*, No. xvii. John Donne.

their conscious minds, and repressing their instinctive natures. Unfortunately, women too are often expected to follow this way, and both pay a heavy price for their conscious development. It seems possible for most young people to pay this price, though even among these there are some who cannot afford to disregard their real natures, and who in doing so break down and become ill; but for many people in the second half of life it becomes imperative to understand those aspects of themselves which in the struggle for existence and the pursuit of ambition or pleasure they have ruthlessly repressed. There is a marked increase in the cases of mental depression and nervous disturbance round about the age of forty, when the ambitions of youth no longer satisfy, and the ideals and values that have been cherished no longer seem of such lustre and importance.

The problem of the second half of life is to find a new meaning and purpose in living, and this, perhaps strangely enough, is best found in the neglected, inferior, and undeveloped side of the personality. Many people, however, cannot face such a possibility, and prefer to cling to the values of youth, and even pursue them in an exaggerated fashion; for them the concept of individuation can have no meaning.

The individuation process is sometimes described as a psychological journey; it can be a tortuous and slippery path, and can at times simply seem to lead round in circles; experience has shown, however, that a truer description would be that of a spiral. In this journey the traveller must first meet with his shadow, and learn to live with this formidable and often terrifying aspect of himself: there is no wholeness without a recognition of the opposites. He will meet, too, with the archetypes of the collective unconscious, and face the danger of succumbing to their peculiar fascination. If he is fortunate he will in the end find 'the treasure hard to attain', the diamond body, the Golden Flower, the lapis, or whatever name and guise have been chosen to designate the archetype of wholeness, the self. One cannot be certain that the goal will be reached, there are too many hazards by the way:

Although everything is experienced in image form, i.e., symbolically, it is by no means a question of fictitious dangers but of very real risks upon which the fate of a whole life may depend. The chief danger is that of succumbing to the fascinating influence of the archetypes. If we do, we may come to a standstill either in a symbolic situation or in an identification with an archetypal personality.[1]

This is what has already been described as an inflation.

The unconscious can only become known by experience, when it is then no longer unconscious in the true sense of the word, but presents itself as strange, wild, chaotic, and apparently meaningless ideas, fantasies, dreams, and visions, which can appear from time to time, or burst upon a person like a flood. Anyone experiencing this is likely to fear that they are going mad, which is why the presence of an analyst – someone who has seen this kind of thing happen before and knows that it need not necessarily or permanently overwhelm consciousness, someone moreover who can provide analogies and say with confidence 'men have been here before, and won something of value from the experience' – can have a calming and helpful effect.

It is absolutely necessary [says Jung] to supply these fantastic images that rise up so strange and threatening before the mind's eye with a sort of context so as to make them more intelligible. The psychological elucidation of these images, which cannot be passed over in silence or blindly ignored, leads logically into the depths of religious phenomenology. The history of religion in its widest sense (including therefore mythology, folklore, and primitive psychology) is a treasure house of archetypal forms from which the doctor can draw helpful parallels and enlightening comparisons for the purpose of calming and clarifying a consciousness that is all at sea.[2]

Jung makes much use of mythological parallels for this purpose; he also discovered the unexpected affinity between individual dream symbolism and medieval alchemy.

Alchemy is popularly regarded as superstitious nonsense,

1. *The Integration of the Personality*, p. 90, cf. *The Archetypes and the Collective Unconscious*, p. 39.
2. *Psychology and Alchemy*, pp. 33, 32.

or at best as a curious interlude preceding the development of the science of chemistry. It is scarcely known that it was taken seriously by such men as Thomas Aquinas, Isaac Newton, and Robert Boyle, and that it had important connexions both with medieval philosophy and with religion. The alchemist is understood as one who tries to make gold, and certainly there were many of this type, but there were equally many others – high-minded and intelligent men – for whom the chemical processes they followed were largely symbolic, and the end in view was not the creation of gold, but the discovery of the philosopher's stone. This mysterious stone – containing the whole secret of the 'art' – was on the one hand a product of their work and on the other a gift from God without which alchemy could not exist; it both held a spirit and was considered to be the spirit itself. In searching for it the alchemist was endeavouring to liberate the spirit he believed to be concealed in matter, and in so doing preserved the bridge to nature – i.e. the unconscious psyche – which the Church, with its emphasis on its sinfulness, was steadily destroying.

The alchemists thought of themselves as good Christians, but they were like many moderns in preferring to seek knowledge through their own experience, rather than to accept by faith what tradition insists on. They used their chemical processes to promote visions, and they recorded their experiences in symbols which have many counterparts in the dreams of to-day.[1]

There are other parallels to be drawn between the alchemical and the analytical process, though the latter has no need of furnaces and retorts, but '[when a patient dreams that] a pot is set upon the fire, then one knows that transformation is under way'.[2]

It is not enough, however, simply to have remarkable dreams or strange experiences; there are those who have a

---

1. Some 400 of such dreams are studied by Jung in *Psychology and Alchemy*.

2. *The Integration of the Personality*, p. 94, 'Archetypes of the Collective Unconscious', Collected Works, Vol. 9.

luxuriant fantasy life without any positive results – quite the opposite, in fact. Anyone can experience the archetypes in dreams, even those of the self, without a corresponding development of personality; it is as if something flowered in the night and withered by day without producing any seed. Whereas the person who has started willingly, or unwillingly, on the way must cherish and cultivate whatever strange, grotesque, or beautiful growths appear. He must work on his material, describing, painting, or modelling it, striving by every means to bring it into a form where it can be contemplated and studied, and its hidden meaning discerned. In this way the work of the analyst can be compared to the opus of the alchemist, and the transformation that he hopes will come about to the alchemical transmutation.

Jung has also made use of analogies from the East, particularly from China, in his work and in his writing. It was in fact contact with Richard Wilhelm the sinologist that first led him to formulate the concept of individuation, and in collaboration the two published *The Secret of the Golden Flower*. In this book the close parallels between a method of Chinese mysticism and the experiences of the patients on the path to individuation were explored. The Chinese philosophy on which the method of meditation described in the text of *The Golden Flower* depends is 'to a certain extent, the common property of all Chinese trends of thought. It is built on the premise that cosmos and man in the last analysis obey common laws; that man is a cosmos in miniature and is not divided from the great cosmos by any fixed limits. The same laws rule for the one as for the other, and from the one a way leads into the other. The psyche and the cosmos are related to each other like the inner and outer worlds. Therefore man participates by nature in all cosmic events, and is inwardly as well as outwardly interwoven with them. Tao, then, the meaning of the world, the way, dominates man just as it does invisible and visible nature (Heaven and Earth).'[1]

'Tao the undivided, Great *One*, gives rise to two opposite

1. *The Secret of the Golden Flower*, Wilhelm and Jung, p. 11.

reality principles, Darkness and Light, Yin and Yang,' and it is the method of reconciling these opposites with which the *Golden Flower* meditation is concerned.[1]

And what of the person who has passed through the ordeal of the individuation process? Of this Jung says:

> It is as if a river that had run to waste in sluggish side-streams and marshes suddenly found its way back to its proper bed, or as if a stone lying on a germinating seed were lifted away so that the shoot could begin its natural growth.[2]

The personality is liberated, healed, and transformed and becomes individual in the fullest sense of the word, but not however individualistic.

1. *The Secret of the Golden Flower*, Wilhelm and Jung, p. 73.
2. *The Development of Personality*, p. 184.

CHAPTER 5

Psychotherapy

PSYCHOTHERAPY is the treatment of the mind, or rather the psyche, by psychological methods. Psychotherapy has come to be identified in the public mind with 'psychoanalysis', a word which was coined by Freud and should strictly speaking be applied only to his method, which explains psychic symptoms in terms of repressed infantile sexual impulses; this implies tracing neuroses back to their roots in infancy.[1] Another widely used method – namely, that of Alfred Adler – explains neurosis in terms of a drive for power, which has arisen as an attempt to compensate for feelings of inferiority, and is known as 'Individual Psychology'.

Jung uses the term Analytical Psychology[2] to describe his own approach, which is not only a way of healing, but also of developing the personality through the individuation process. Since, however, individuation is not the goal of all who seek psychological help, and in many cases more limited aims are indicated, he varies his treatment according to the age, state of development, and temperament of his patients, and does not neglect either the sexual urge or the will to power, if these are operative factors in the neurosis.

He considers that the divergent views on the 'right' method of psychotherapy arise, in large part, from the

1. When Jung worked out his own approach in contrast to that of Freud this was correct, hence it has been stated in this form. More recently the Freudian School, and notably that branch of it influenced by the work of Melanie Klein, has come to regard difficulties in mastering the infant's aggressive impulses as the more important cause of neurosis.

2. To avoid confusion with G. F. Stout's term 'Analytic Psychology' (as distinct from Analytical Psychology), Jung's psychology has recently been re-named 'Complex Psychology'. The term 'Analytical Psychology' is, however, better known, and is in fact current usage. Stout uses the word analytic in a different sense.

widely differing view-point of the extravert and the introvert. Seen in this light, Freud's psychology would be extraverted, for he considered that the prime cause of neurosis was the frustration of the infantile sexual impulse (using the term 'sexual' in the widest sense) which arose necessarily from outside. Adler, on the other hand, put the emphasis on an inner drive for power, which in his experience caused neurosis when it 'got out of hand' and interfered with the normal social functioning of the individual.

It would certainly have never occurred to me [says Jung] to depart from Freud's path had I not stumbled upon facts which forced me into modifications. And the same is true of my relation to the Adlerian viewpoint. ... It seems hardly necessary to add that I hold the truth of my own views to be equally relative, and feel myself ... the mere exponent of another disposition.[1]

Jung does not neglect either the sexual urge or the will to power, if these are operative factors in the neurosis, but he finds that the Freudian or Adlerian points of view are usually most appropriate to young people. At this stage of life a man or woman needs to give the instincts the importance that is their due, and yet allow them to function in a way that society will accept; sexuality and the need for self-assertion are the primary urges at this period. Material and worldly success, and especially intellectual success, is often won at the expense of the sexual urge, and when this causes a neurosis, it is most likely to be helped by interpretation of the difficulties in terms of their infantile sexual sources. On the other hand, the unsuccessful person who attempts to compensate for this with self-assertion needs to see the fictitious nature of his aims.

At the same time Jung never loses sight of the constructive elements which he knows can always be found in a neurosis. To work only backward and downwards – i.e. looking for traumas in infancy – can have a destructive rather than a healing effect, and for this reason he is never content merely to find the causes of the trouble. An excellent example of

1. *The Practice of Psychotherapy*, p. 37, 'The Aims of Psychotherapy', Collected Works, Vol. 16.

this twofold way of regarding a neurosis is to be found in the case of a young man who came to Jung for the treatment of homosexuality, one of the causes of which was a too-intense relationship to his mother. The young man had two dreams, one preceding, one immediately after his first interview, in which there was no attempt at dream analysis. They were:

(1) I am in a lofty cathedral filled with mysterious twilight. They tell me that it is the cathedral at Lourdes. In the centre there is a deep dark well, into which I have to descend. (2) I am in a great Gothic cathedral. At the altar stands a priest. I stand before him with my friend, holding in my hand a little Japanese ivory figure, with the feeling that it is going to be baptized. Suddenly an elderly woman appears, takes the fraternity ring from my friend's finger, and puts it on her own. My friend is afraid that this may bind him in some way. But at the same moment there is a sound of wonderful organ music.

Of these dreams Jung says:

They show the patient's situation in a highly remarkable light, and one that is very strange to the conscious mind, while at the same time lending to the banal medical situation an aspect that is uniquely attuned to the mental peculiarities of the dreamer, and thus capable of stringing his aesthetic, intellectual, and religious interests to concert pitch. No better conditions for treatment could possibly be imagined.[1]

For a detailed analysis of these dreams the reader is referred to Jung's own work,[2] but even one unskilled in dream interpretation may catch something of their atmosphere and meaning. The reference to healing, i.e. Lourdes, the place of healing, is unmistakable, and the suggestion that an ordeal is to be faced before a change can take place is also clear. It seems, too, as if the whole experience is to be taken in a religious spirit. This is in striking contrast to the usual sordid associations of homosexuality. In the second dream the young man associated the ivory figure with *membrum virile*

1. *Two Essays on Analytical Psychology*, pp. 101, 105, 107.
2. *Ibid.*, pp. 100–7.

and its baptism with the Jewish rite of circumcision which was he said 'a sort of baptism'. It seems then as if the sexual organ is to be baptized; in other words, *dedicated to a new purpose*, especially since a priest is present at the ceremony. Jung at this point draws many analogies with rites of initiation, all of which have the purpose of leading young men out of a childish state into a participation with the adult world. Lastly the ring is taken from the friend (the one with whom he has been homosexually connected) and given to a woman. It is true that this elderly lady had a motherly aspect, and one might perhaps conclude that this was therefore merely a regression – i.e. the wish for an incestuous relationship with a mother – but the dream closed on a positive note with the beautiful organ music, and left the young man with a feeling of harmony and peace. There is therefore justification for thinking that the placing of the ring on the lady's finger indicated a step forward towards a heterosexual rather than a homosexual attitude. This, in fact, proved to be the case, and these dreams therefore showed the possibility of a development which might unfold in the right atmosphere. To have traced merely the causes of this neurosis would have been to neglect, perhaps even to destroy unconscious forces working towards its cure.[1]

When older people (say those over forty) become neurotic they need treating in quite a different manner from the young. This is especially true if their life has been reasonably successful up to the time when the neurosis develops. There is in addition a type of middle-aged patient who is not neurotic in the ordinary sense, but who simply finds life empty and meaningless. This is not a clinically definable neurosis, but might well be described as 'the general neurosis of our times'. Quite a third of Jung's patients come from this class of person, and it is therefore natural that his special contribution to psychotherapy should be seen most clearly in relation to this type of case.

1. N.B. It may be added that the development indicated in the dreams did not come about immediately, or by any means easily, and that without the positive sign they gave there were times during the treatment when pessimism might have ruled.

In Jung's view every neurosis has an aim; it is an attempt to compensate for a one-sided attitude to life, and a voice, as it were, drawing attention to a side of personality that has been neglected or repressed.

'The symptoms of a neurosis are not simply the effects of long past causes, whether infantile sexuality or the infantile urge to power, they are also attempts at a new synthesis of life – unsuccessful attempts let it be added – yet attempts nevertheless, with a core of value and meaning.'[1] This is where Jung's own particular contribution to psychotherapy appears: firstly, his insistence that a neurosis should not be regarded as something entirely negative, but that if it can be understood, a hint of new possibilities of development will be found in it; secondly, in his view that there are other important drives in human nature besides those of sexuality and self-assertion, and that the cultural or spiritual drive is, in the second half of life, of more importance than the other two. A further distinction Jung makes is that the causes of a neurosis are to be found in the present as well as in the past (the past is significant only if it is clearly having an effect on the present) and in the failure of the libido to carry the person over some obstacle and on to a new stage of development. These are points where all rational explanations or conscious attempts at adjustment fail, and where hope lies only in tapping the energy of the unconscious, and releasing new sources of life. This has already been referred to in the chapter on Individuation, and will be returned to as it is of first importance both in understanding Analytical Psychology and in assessing the contribution it makes to life. In the meantime it is necessary to describe the general therapeutic process in more detail.

A neurosis is a particular kind of psychic disturbance which interferes with the life, and often with the health, of the person suffering from it. In Jung's view it is caused by a conflict between two tendencies; one expressed consciously, the other by a complex split off from consciousness and lead-

1. *Two Essays on Analytical Psychology*, p. 45.

ing an independent but unconscious existence. This complex may or may not have been previously conscious; the point is that the neurotic does not know that it exists; but it interferes, either by obtruding unexpectedly into consciousness or by attracting energy to itself, so that less and less is available for conscious and directed activity.

A neurosis may show itself in the mildest way, in fact we are all sufferers to some extent; most of our lapses of speech or of memory, misunderstandings of what we have heard or read, or of other people's motives, or so-called hallucinations of memory when we mistakenly believe we have done or have not done something, are neurotic in origin. At the other extreme lie the dramatic cases of lost memory, hysterical paralysis, blindness, or deafness, &c. – i.e. physical conditions for which there is no traceable physical cause – and in between the host of anxieties, fears, and obsessions from which the wretched sufferer is quite unable to free himself. Many apparently inexplicable illnesses, headaches, fevers, and so on, are neurotic. For example, we may cite the case of a man with a high temperature which went down immediately to normal after he had been able to make a full confession of a dark and forgotten secret.[1] Confession is, in fact, of first importance in any analytical treatment:

> The first beginnings of all analytical treatment of the soul [says Jung] are to be found in its prototype, the confessional. Since, however, the two have no direct causal connexion, but rather grow from a common irrational psychic root, it is difficult for an outsider to see at once the relation between the groundwork of psychoanalysis and the religious institution of the confessional.[2]
> Once the human mind had succeeded in inventing the idea of sin, man had recourse to psychic concealment – or in analytical parlance, repression arose.[3]

This is the common psychic root – the fact that men conceal things, and in so doing alienate themselves from the

1. *Two Essays on Analytical Psychology.*
2. *The Practice of Psychotherapy*, p. 55, 'Problems of Modern Psychotherapy'.
3. *Ibid.*, p. 55.

community. What is concealed tends to be everything 'dark, imperfect, and stupid in ourselves', and so the secret is laden with guilt, whether or no it is something really wrong from the standpoint of ordinary morality. In fact one form of concealment, which can have a most damaging effect, is often practised as a virtue – that is the concealment of emotion. In both cases, however, a reservation must be made; some secrets are necessary to our development as individuals and prevent us from becoming dissolved in the unconsciousness of community life, and the control of emotion is necessary and desirable if carried out in the right way. Self-restraint as a merely private virtue leads to 'the well known bad moods and irritability of the over-virtuous'.[1] It also damages personal relationships, leading to coldness where there should be warmth, a false air of superiority, or a tepid harmony. Self-restraint, in fact, needs to be practised for social or religious ends, not for personal aggrandizement or from fear.

A full confession – that is to say, 'not merely the intellectual recognition of the facts with the head, but their confirmation by the heart, and the actual release of suppressed emotion'[2] – can have a wonderfully healing effect, especially with uncomplicated people. But unfortunately confession is not a simple matter, for the personality of the confessor plays an important part in obtaining the right effect. It also frequently happens that, though the patient is apparently cured, insofar as his symptoms have been removed by confession, or that he now understands their origin and meaning, he persists in continuing his treatment, even though there is no apparent necessity for this. He cannot do without the one who cured him.

It has been found (and this was Freud's special contribution) that this obstinate attachment to the analyst is the result of the patient having transferred to him or her feelings which were once given to the real parents, or in psychologi-

1. *The Practice of Psychotherapy*, p. 58, 'Problems of Modern Psychotherapy'.
2. *Ibid.*, p. 41.

cal terms 'the memory-image of the father and mother with its accent of feeling is transferred to the analyst', hence the name 'transference' is given to the phenomena. The patient has become like a child, or rather he was like a child all the time, but he suppressed this fact; now he tries to reproduce with the analyst the family situations of childhood. Most often the analyst represents the parent of the opposite sex, but brother–sister, father–son, and mother–daughter relationships may also appear. In this phase much that has been repressed comes into the daylight, and many fantasies appear, especially fantasies of incest. It is therefore not surprising that these had previously remained unconscious, and that it is not easy to become conscious of such contents or of other unsavoury matters which may be unearthed. The forces that become active during this stage of analysis are predominatingly erotic, but what Adler has called 'the will to power' can also be active. The patient then uses his childishness to try to dominate the situation and exploits his neurosis to gain importance. The patient only becomes aware of these things through 'the interpretation of the transference' – i.e. an explanation of what is happening in his relationship to the analyst, and this explanation needs to be given afresh at every stage, for the transference naturally develops and changes.

'Explanation' is perhaps a misleading word to describe what is both a method and a process, for the emotions are deeply involved. The transference cannot be explained away; it has to be lived through with the analyst. Though limitations are imposed by the conditions of the consulting-room and the restrictions of fixed hours of treatment, Jung insists that the analyst should meet the patient as a fellow human being, that if necessary there should be equal frankness between them, and that any suffering should be shared. From this relationship of two people spring therapeutic results which no mere explanation could effect.

It is this same human relationship which makes the personality of the analyst so important in obtaining relief through confession. It may also happen that the patient

becomes aware of a split-off part of the personality – an auto-
nomous complex – and yet has the greatest difficulty in inte-
grating it, since it expresses something absolutely contra-
dictory to the conscious personality. At this point the understanding and sympathy of the analyst are of the utmost importance, helping to reinforce the powers of consciousness
until it is able to assimilate the disturbing factor. The patient
does not then 'stand alone in his battle with these elemental
powers, but someone whom he trusts reaches out a hand,
lending him moral strength to combat the tyranny of uncontrolled emotion'.[1] If, however, there is to be this close relationship it is of the greatest importance that the analyst
himself should first have been analysed,[2] for he cannot help
another person to a stage farther than he has reached himself. The analyst must know his own shadow and have had
real experience of the unconscious forces which he is now
helping his patient to face. He cannot evade his own difficulties by trying to cure other people; he must first cure
himself. In sharing his patients' experiences he risks becoming infected by their illness (just as a doctor may be infected
by physical illness), and he needs all the stability that self-
knowledge can bring.

In all his discussions on Psychotherapy, Jung emphasizes
the fact that it rests on the relationship between two human
beings; this is the significant thing to which all theories and
methods should be secondary. The analyst cannot sometimes
prevent himself from thinking that this, that, or the other
course would be best for the patient, but he has no right to
impose his views; his business is to help the patient towards
that state where he can discover for himself the way to live
and the necessary impetus to put this into practice. Theories
and methods are only aids towards this end.

There are many stages at which psychological treatment
can come to an end: when, for instance, disagreeable symptoms have disappeared; when there has been a satisfactory

1. *The Practice of Psychotherapy*, p. 132.
2. It was Jung who first saw this clearly and Freud was quick to
agree.

development from a childish state, or when a new and better adaptation to life has been achieved; or again when an essential but unconscious psychic content has been realized and a new impetus given to life. But there are some people who find no permanent satisfaction in these solutions, and who either continue their work with the analyst, or return at some later date, driven by the desire for further understanding and development. There are also those more or less normal people who, having reached the second half of life, are dissatisfied, and being unable to find comfort in the ordinary ways, turn to analysis to see if it can provide any solution of their difficulties. These are the people to whom the goal of individuation is a necessity, and the ordinary psychotherapeutic processes scarcely apply. In fact, Jung calls this stage of analysis a 'dialectical discussion between the conscious mind and the unconscious, a development or an advance towards some goal or end the perplexing nature of which has engaged my attention for many years'.[1] Most of the patients to whom this applies have led well-adapted and often successful lives; many of them have had some form of psychotherapeutic treatment 'with partial or negative results',[2] and most of them complain of the emptiness or lack of meaning in their lives, or express themselves as 'being stuck', or of having no idea what they shall do or where they shall turn. They are often able and intelligent people to whom normalization means nothing; in fact their neurosis (if such it can be called) lies in their 'normality' and their deepest need is to be able to live 'abnormal lives'.

To be a normal human being is probably the most useful and fitting thing of which we can think; but the very notion of a 'normal human being', like the concept of adaptation, implies a restriction to the average ... To be 'normal' is the ideal aim for the unsuccessful, for all those who are still below the general level of adaptation. But for people of more than average ability, people who never found it difficult to gain successes and to accomplish their share of the world's work – for them the moral

1. *Psychology and Alchemy*, p. 4.
2. *The Practice of Psychotherapy*, p. 41, 'The Aims of Psychotherapy'.

compulsion to be nothing but normal signifies the bed of Procrustes – deadly and insupportable boredom, a hell of sterility and hopelessness.[1]

Both these people, and those whose chief difficulty lies in having come to a 'dead end', have often read widely, thought deeply, and explored all the possibilities offered by religion and philosophy; they know all the answers that consciousness can give. It is at this point that Jung makes his most significant contribution to psychotherapy.

I have no ready-made philosophy of life to hand out. ... I do not know what to say to the patient when he asks me, 'What do you advise? What shall I do?' I don't know either. I only know one thing: when my conscious mind no longer sees any possible road ahead and consequently gets stuck, my unconscious psyche will react to the unbearable standstill.[2]

This coming to a standstill is such a familiar human situation, and has so often been repeated in the history of mankind, that it has become the theme of many a fairy-tale and myth of the 'Open Sesame' type, where the locked door opens to the magic words, or the hidden way is revealed by some helpful animal or strange creature. 'Getting stuck' is one of those typical events 'which in the course of time have evoked typical reactions and compensations'.[3] It is quite likely, therefore, that when this psychic situation is repeated in the life of modern man his unconscious will react to it with a dream of a similar type.

The aim of therapy at this stage is for the patient to explore the latent possibilities in himself, to find out what kind of a person he really is, and to learn to live accordingly. The analyst must therefore set aside all preconceived ideas as to the way his patient should develop, and the emphasis lies not on 'treatment', but on the relationship between analyst and patient, for neither knows the answer or can predict the outcome. 'By no device,' says Jung 'can the treatment be any-

1. *The Practice of Psychotherapy*, p. 70, 'Problems of Modern Psychotherapy'.
2. *Ibid.*, pp. 41–2, 'The Aims of Psychotherapy'.
3. *Ibid.*, p. 42.

thing but the product of mutual influence, in which the whole being of the doctor as well as that of his patient plays its part.'[1]

Between doctor and patient, therefore, there are imponderable factors which bring about a mutual transformation. In the process, the stronger and more stable personality will decide the final issue. I have seen many cases where the patient assimilated the doctor in defiance of all theory and of the latter's professional intentions. ... The stage of transformation is grounded on these facts.[2]

Jung has likened this meeting of two personalities to the contact of two chemical substances; if there is any reaction both are transformed. Nor is this a fanciful or vague analogy, for it formed part of the basis of Jung's researches into Alchemy.[3] This process (i.e. that of mutual transformation) demands as much of the analyst as it does of the patient, the same honesty and perseverance, the same readiness for change; and it makes heavy demands on him, for in the last resort it is always his own personality rather than a method or technique which is the determining factor.

If the patient's problem is a religious one, then the analyst must face his religious problems too, and, what is more, he must be able to discuss them frankly with his patient. If the patient's task is one of higher cultural development, then the analyst must also develop in this way.

Psychotherapy [as Jung says] transcends its medical origins and ceases to be merely a method for treating the sick. It now treats the healthy or such as have a moral right to psychic health, whose sickness is at most the suffering that torments us all.

The earlier stages of analysis deal largely with personal problems, and therefore with the personal unconscious, but

1. *The Practice of Psychotherapy*, p. 71, 'Problems of Modern Psychotherapy'.
2. *Ibid.*, p. 72.
3. Cf. *The Practice of Psychotherapy*, 'Psychology of the Transference'.
4. *The Practice of Psychotherapy*, p. 75, 'Problems of Modern Psychotherapy'.

the last stage, in which the individual needs to find his place in the life of the generations, touches the collective unconscious, and it is Jung's theory of a collective as well as a personal unconscious that differentiates his psychology from all others.

CHAPTER 6

Dreams and their Interpretation

MUCH has been said about dreams in the previous chapters – enough probably to show how important Jung regards them as a manifestation of psychic activity. A dream, he says, should 'be regarded with due seriousness as an actuality that has to be fitted into the conscious attitude as a co-determining factor',[1] and his experience has shown him that 'if we meditate on a dream sufficiently long and thoroughly, if we carry it around with us and turn it over and over, something almost always comes of it'.[2]

A dream is an involuntary and spontaneous psychic product, a voice of nature; and is usually obscure and difficult to understand because it expresses itself in symbols and pictures, like the most ancient writing, or the complicated letters which children sometimes enjoy producing with drawings replacing the important words. In attempting to understand the dream-language, Jung uses a method of amplification, which may be compared in some respects to the way in which inscriptions and writings in forgotten languages are deciphered by the philologist.

The first step in understanding a dream, he considers, is to establish its context. This means unravelling its network of relationships with the dreamer and his or her life, and discovering the significance of the various images it presents. For example, one's mother might appear in a dream: now, everyone has a concept of what mother implies, but for each person the image of a mother is different, and the significance of this image will even vary from time to time. The thought of mother may for one person be associated with love, care, and protection, and for another with power, anger,

1. *The Practice of Psychotherapy*, p. 153, 'The Practical Use of Dream-Analysis'.
2. *Ibid.*, p. 42, 'Aims of Psychotherapy'.

or frustration and so the meaning of a dream of mother can vary accordingly. As far as possible, each image or symbol must be taken in turn till its meaning for the dreamer is established as nearly as possible, and not until this has been carefully done is one in a position to understand what the dream may mean. It will be seen from this that Jung does not have a fixed method of dream interpretation (one cannot say, for instance, as the popular dream-books do, that to dream of black cats means good luck), for each dream is taken as a direct expression of the dreamer's unconscious, and only to be understood in this light.

Jung's way of dealing with dreams differs from the method of free association,[1] which, as he says, will help to uncover complexes, but not necessarily complexes connected with the dream; in fact, free association will usually lead away from the dream altogether.

When somebody dreams of a 'deal table', it is not enough for him to associate it with his writing-desk which does not happen to be made of deal. Supposing that nothing more occurs to the dreamer, this blocking has an objective meaning, for it indicates that a particular darkness reigns in the immediate neighbourhood of the dream-image, and that is suspicious. We would expect him to have dozens of associations to a deal table, and the fact that there is apparently nothing is itself significant. In such cases I keep on returning to the image, and I usually say to my patient, 'Suppose I had no idea what the words "deal table" mean. Describe this object and give me its history in such a way that I cannot fail to understand what sort of a thing it is.' In this way we manage to establish almost the whole context of the dream-image. When we have done this for all the images in the dream we are ready for the venture of interpretation.[2]

A series of dreams makes a more satisfactory basis for interpretation than a single dream, for the theme which the unconscious is presenting becomes clearer, the important images are underlined by repetition, and mistakes in interpretation are corrected by the next dream.

1. In 'free association' a chain of random associations is followed wherever they may lead.

2. *The Practice of Psychotherapy*, pp. 149–50, 'The Practical Use of Dream-Analysis'.

Dreams and their Interpretations

Dreams can be interpreted on an objective or on a subjective level. In the first case the dream is related to what is going on in the environment; the people appearing in it are taken as real, and their relationship to, and possible influence on the dreamer are analysed. In the second case the dream-figures are taken as representing aspects of the dreamer's personality. It depends on the circumstances of the moment which side the emphasis shall be placed. A woman dreaming of her father may need to face a problem connected with him or some aspect of her relationship to him, or she may need to recognize the male principle (personified by the father) in herself. Generally speaking, the subjective aspect of dreams becomes more important in the later stages of analysis when the personal problems have been seen and understood.

Some dreams have considerably more than personal significance; such dreams are often vivid, and make use of surprising and even incomprehensible symbols, and their relationship to the dreamer is difficult to trace. These Jung classes as collective dreams, and to understand them use must often be made of historical and mythological analogies to find what the symbols meant to other men in other times. It may seem strange at first to think that these could have any relevance to ourselves; we have cut ourselves off from the past to such an extent that it is difficult to realize that the experiences of remote people can still have meaning for us. Yet it is so; unconsciously we still think like our distant ancestors, and to understand this is to deepen our experience, open up new possibilities, and give us the stability and vigour which come from discovering our roots.

It is difficult to make the distinction between personal and collective dreams clear without going into more detail than is possible here. In any case, there is, just as in life, no sharp line of demarcation between the two. Whatever we think or do in a personal capacity has some meaning for or influence on other people; conversely, we also belong to our time and milieu, which shape us, whether we will or no. Strictly speaking, a personal dream would arise from the personal

99

unconscious and be concerned with the personal aspects of the dreamer's life: dreams of one's family, friends, and daily happenings are of this nature.

A collective dream[1] will, however, present archetypes from the collective unconscious and have significance for others as well as the dreamer. There is probably some reader who has told such a dream at the breakfast table, and noticed its effect upon the hearers, for the archetypes always have a certain impact upon people. A collective dream has, however, considerably greater significance than any immediate dramatic effect it may have. Primitive people instinctively recognize the difference between these two kinds of dreams, personal and collective, and describe them as little and big dreams, prizing the latter, for they often tap sources of knowledge which would otherwise be closed. An interesting example is given by Rasmussen in a book on the Polar Eskimos, where one of the tribe had a vision in a dream, and because of this led the others for many days over the ice to a new place, where there was food and shelter, just as the dream had foretold. Some, however, lost faith during the journey, and these turned back, only to perish from starvation, as had also been foretold.

The collective dream was highly valued in antiquity when it was accepted as having an oracular nature and its warnings taken seriously. These dreams and their interpretation appear fanciful to us now; nevertheless, there are some parallels which we can draw with the principles of interpretation we use to-day. Pharoah's dream, recorded in Genesis 41, and its interpretation by Joseph, is a collective dream of this type: 'And it came to pass at the end of two full years that Pharoah dreamed.'

The king's dreams were of supreme importance to the people, for Pharaoh was both god and the land's representative among the gods. He was the official intermediary between the gods and the people, so that his dreams were as the voice of god conveyed to the people. It did not seem

1. Jung quotes many of these dreams in his various works, and analyses a series of them in *The Integration of the Personality.*

necessary, however, that Pharaoh should interpret his dreams, for in this case he sent for the magicians, who were unfortunately quite at a loss to understand the message. Then Pharaoh sent for Joseph, who had previously shown his skill in dream interpretation with two of Pharaoh's servants.

And Pharaoh said unto Joseph, 'In my dream, behold, I stood upon the bank of the river. And, behold, there came up out of the river seven kine, fat-fleshed and well-favoured; and they fed in a meadow. And, behold, seven other kine came up after them, poor and very ill-favoured and lean-fleshed, such as I never saw in all the land of Egypt for badness. And the lean and the ill-favoured kine did eat up the first seven fat kine; and when they had eaten them up, it could not be known that they had eaten them; but they were still ill-favoured, as at the beginning. So I awoke. And I saw in my dreams, and, behold, seven ears came up in one stalk, full and good. And, behold, seven ears, withered, thin, and blasted with the east wind, sprung up after them. And the thin ears devoured the seven good ears: and I told this unto the magicians: but there was none that could declare it to me.'

Both corn and kine had tremendous significance for the Egyptians, expressed in their myths and religious ceremonies, and with a symbolic meaning reaching beyond the everyday one of food to death, re-birth, creation, &c., and as such archetypal.[1] Joseph's understanding of the dreams appears to be intuitive; earlier (when consulted by Pharaoh's butler and baker), he has said: 'Do not interpretations belong to God?' and now he says, 'It is not in me: God shall give Pharaoh an answer of peace'. And then: 'The dream of Pharaoh is one. God hath showed Pharaoh what he is about to do. The seven good kine are seven years; and the seven good ears are seven years; the dream is one.'

We should make a similar statement about dream material to-day, for, as has been pointed out in previous chapters, the unconscious constantly uses different symbols for what consciousness regards as one and the same thing.

1. Osiris was the Egyptian god of the corn. There were also sacred bulls who were dedicated to him and ordained to be worshipped as gods. Frazer, *The Golden Bough*.

Joseph continues:

And the seven thin and ill-favoured kine that came up after them are seven years; and the seven empty ears blasted with the east wind shall be seven years of famine. This is the thing which I have spoken unto Pharaoh. What God is about to do he showeth unto Pharaoh. Behold, there come seven years of great plenty throughout all the land of Egypt; and there shall arise after them seven years of famine; and all the plenty shall be forgotten in the land of Egypt, and the famine shall consume the land. And the plenty shall not be known in the land by reason of that famine following; for it shall be very grievous. And for that the dream was doubled unto Pharaoh twice; it is because the thing is established by God, and God will shortly bring it to pass.

We have already said that a series of dreams are easier to understand than a single dream, and in the same way we find to-day that important dreams are repeated if they have not been understood, or if they need to be emphasized.

The Bible story finishes with Joseph's plans to meet the crisis and Pharaoh's acceptance of them. The succeeding events showed how correct his interpretation had been for both the years of plenty and the famine came just as he had predicted from the dreams.

To ancient man the dream was sent by God, and while the Church still allows this possibility (only very cautiously, and reserving to itself the right to adjudicate in the matter), popular opinion to-day has deprecated this kind of psychic activity to such an extent that it is often believed that dreams are merely the result of physical causes, such as sleeping in an uncomfortable position, or eating a heavy meal before going to bed. Some dreams, it is true, can be traced to such causes (if, for instance, we dream we are walking in the snow and wake to find the bed-clothes have slipped off), but frequently there is little connexion between the stimulus and the form the dream takes, so that it is not an explanation of the dream in any real sense. Another fairly common belief is that dreams reproduce the events of the day before, especially if these were significant or striking. Careful recording, however, shows that dreams rarely repeat events in an exact manner; they add or subtract something, round off the experience, or can be shown to be compensatory in character. This tendency to compensate a conscious attitude is an important characteristic of the dream, and must always be taken into account when attempting to understand it. As an example of this, Jung quotes a young man who dreamt his father was behaving in a drunken and disorderly manner. The real father did no such thing, and, according to the son, behaved in a somewhat ideal way. The young man had an excellent relationship with him – too good, in fact, for his admiration of his father prevented him from having the necessary confidence in himself and developing his own different personality.[1] In this case the dream went to the other extreme, showing the father in a most unfavourable light. It was almost as if the dream were saying, 'He is not so marvellous after all, and he can behave in a quite irresponsible manner. There is no need for you to feel so inferior.' The unconscious was drawing attention to a relationship based on an idealistic view of the father which was hindering the son's growth into manhood.

Dreams also work the other way round; if we habitually undervalue somebody, we are likely to have a highly flattering dream about him, to see him, for instance, in a much higher position than the one he would normally occupy, or doing something with ease and skill where we know we should be incompetent and clumsy.

Dreams also bring hidden conflicts to light by showing an unknown side of the character, as when a mild, inoffensive person dreams of violence, or an ascetic of sexual orgies, but more frequently the dream-language is less direct than this. For instance, there are hosts of sexual symbols well known in myth as well as dream: 'the bull, the ass, the pomegranate, the horse's hoof, the dance, to mention only a few'.[2]

Dreams sometimes express hidden wishes, but it is too simple to class them all under this heading. The 'wish'

1. *The Practice of Psychotherapy*, pp. 154-5, 'The Practical Use of Dream-Analysis'.
2. *Ibid.*, p. 157.

dream is usually easy to spot; when, for instance, the hungry man dreams he is eating a wonderful meal, or the thirsty that they see sparkling water.

There are also forward-looking or 'prospective' dreams. It seems, indeed, as if space and time are creations of our consciousness, and are relative, and the unconscious does not work according to these concepts.

. A simple example of the 'prospective' dream is that of getting up and dressing, when one is really asleep in bed and the alarm has gone off; but there are others which are more striking than this, like that of the woman who was shortly going to move to a new and unknown district who dreamt correctly all about the house she would live in, down to the smallest detail, even including the reason why its present owners were leaving it. Such dreams are not uncommon; Osbert Sitwell in his autobiography records some interesting examples, but our distrust of this kind of psychic activity usually leads us to dismiss them as 'just coincidence'.

Occasionally dreams seem to be clear warnings of danger, as for example that of the mountain climber who dreamed he was climbing higher and higher and then gaily stepping off into space. One would have thought that such a dream would have made the least superstitious of persons stop to think, but the man in question simply laughed. Not so very long after he was killed in the mountains, a friend actually seeing him step off into the air.[1] To dream of death, however, does not necessarily indicate a fatal accident; there is symbolic as well as actual physical death, as the poets know well – the year dies, the song dies, the lover dies of love, and the mystic dies to life:

> Leave nothing of myself in me;
> Let me so read thy life that I
> Unto all life of mine may die.[2]

Only a knowledge of the dreamer and his immediate circumstances will show on which side the emphasis is rightly placed.

1. *The Practice of Psychotherapy*, p. 151.
2. Richard Crashaw, 'Upon the Book and Picture of the Seraphical Saint Teresa'.

Sometimes dreams reproduce things seen, heard, or read long before and subsequently forgotten, or recall distant experiences. It is often difficult to trace whether a lost memory is really being recalled, or whether the experience actually happened, but this is not of great practical importance; what is relevant is why the dreamer had such a dream at this particular moment, and why he felt he had that particular experience.

One curious feature of dreaming is the way that close friends or members of the same family, particularly husband and wife or parents and children, will dream the same dream without previously having told it to each other. Still more curious is the way that children sometimes have of dreaming about their parents' problems, when these have been carefully hidden from them. The dream is not usually a straightforward statement, but is symbolical and often picturesque in manner. A curious example is that of three girls who had a most devoted mother:

When they were approaching puberty they confessed shame-facedly to each other that for years they had suffered from horrible dreams about [their mother]. They dreamt of her as a witch or a dangerous animal and they could not understand it at all, since their mother was so lovely and utterly devoted to them. Years later the mother became insane and in her insanity crawled about on all fours and imitated the grunting of pigs, the barking of dogs, and the growling of bears.[1]

The most striking dreams are those which seem to arise spontaneously from the unconscious, presenting something completely strange with a vividness that compels attention. Sometimes these seem to express a tendency of the unconscious aiming at a complete change of the conscious attitude, and they can be so impressive that the dreamer is in fact changed by the experience without any interpretation being necessary. An example is the following dream of an intellectually developed woman approaching middle age:

I am in a great empty temple. At one end is a gigantic statue of the god. There is a tall priest in robes with me. The atmosphere is

1. *The Development of Personality*, p. 55, 'Child Development and Education'.

Egyptian or Chinese. We walk over the immense empty floor towards the statue at the end. Every few steps I fall on my face and the priest calls out to the god that I am coming as a penitent and he makes confession for me aloud. Our progress is slow and solemn, but in my own thoughts I am very sceptical about it all. I think this is a queer kind of ritual and that the god over there is only a stone statue. We finally come to it. On each side of it there are steps and we go up these and so behind the altar. Once there and before leaving the temple I turn round to look again at the statue, and as I look it slowly turns round and looks at me. I find myself falling on my face in real awe and devotion at last, for it really is the presence of a god with absolution and grace pouring in on me. Somebody says: 'It's all a trick, there is a machine to turn the statue round.' But I feel passionately that it may be a trick to turn a stone statue round, but all the same it is also a god and I have experienced him. I leave the place with a sense of being illuminated and humbled and glad.

The dream is of value in analytical practice because it gives a picture of inner, and also often of outer conditions of which the dreamer is unaware. The first dream that a patient brings to analysis often gives a striking summing up of his or her problem, and even a hint of how it may be solved. It is this forward-looking aspect of dreams that, among other reasons, leads Jung to insist that they shall not only be used for reductive purposes; that is, dreams do not only uncover forgotten memories and present difficulties, but appear, especially in the case of individuation dreams, to have a goal in view. Dreams at the beginning of analysis are often relatively clear and simple, and have an immediate effect. As an analysis proceeds the dreams usually grow more complicated and difficult to understand. It is at this stage that mythological themes often occur and that a wider framework than that of the dreamer's personal experience and associations becomes necessary. Sometimes the dreamer has no meaningful associations and can find no relationship to the dream situation; it is here that mythological parallels can be helpful. These will usually throw light on the collective meaning of the dream, and its relevance to the dreamer can then be worked out.

Jung never imposes an interpretation on a patient. He looks on it as even more important for the dreamer to understand his own dream than for the analyst to do so, while ideally the interpretation should be the result of mutual reflection and agreement. Much of his work lies in helping patients to deal with their own unconscious material, and they are encouraged to record their dreams carefully, and even to illustrate them either with pictures or models in wax or clay. No artistic ability is needed for this; in fact it is better to approach the work naïvely, for one is less likely to falsify the picture. The expressions of the unconscious are often most primitive, and their power is lost if there is too great an attempt to fit them into aesthetic concepts. By working on dreams in this manner the patient (though he is still likely to overlook unpleasant implications) can develop his independence and learn, to some extent, to understand the unconscious himself. He makes more real the fantasies that are activating him, and so he knows better what they are. Even the mere painting of a picture can have an effect, curing a wretched mood, or bringing a release of tension. Through active co-operation of this kind the danger of floating aimlessly in an endless sea of fantasy is avoided and dreams become, not only sources of information, but also of creative power.

CHAPTER 7

Psychology and Education

JUNG has made an interesting contribution to the understanding of child development in demonstrating, through
the medium of the association tests, how closely the psychology of a child is linked with that of its parents. Even a whole
family can show strikingly similar reactions.[1] Children, as
we have already seen, can have dreams which reflect the
parents' problems, and nervous disturbances or bad behaviour can often be traced to parental difficulties which
have been carefully concealed from the child. If the parents
solve their own problems, or sometimes if they merely bring
their difficulties into the light of day and share them frankly
with the child (naturally on a level that he or she can understand), the child's nervousness or refractoriness will often
disappear as if by magic.

Jung describes the case of a girl of nine who ran a low
temperature for months and was unable to attend school,
though no cause could be found for the condition. The
parents were unhappy together and wished for a divorce,
but could not come to a decision to take the actual step.
They were sure the child knew nothing of this, and that she
was not worried in any way. The child's dreams, however,
showed that she was aware of the situation, and she confessed that whenever her father went away (as he sometimes
did on business trips) she was afraid that he would never come
back. She also noticed that her mother was happier then.
The parents came to see at last that they were making the
child ill by leaving their problem unsolved. They had either
to work out an adjustment between themselves or to separate. They chose the latter, and explained to the child that
she would not be entirely parted from either of them, but

1. *Collected Papers on Analytical Psychology*, pp. 119-32.

would have two homes in future, and though this seems a far from ideal arrangement, the child's relief at being freed from her vague fears and intuitions was so great that she was soon well again and able to return to school.[1]

The close identity of thought in families is sometimes strikingly clear, when each member echoes the opinion of the other and shares the general likes and dislikes, but the unconscious identity of children and parents is less obvious, and usually only shown in dreams and through the medium of tests like the association tests. The unconscious influence of parents can burden a child and hinder its development; for instance, a wife dissatisfied with her husband may unknowingly heap on her son the emotion that would normally flow towards the father, and a father may be really in love with his little daughter, and jealously prevent any other influence entering her life. The story of the early life of Elizabeth Barrett Browning is a good, if extreme, example of the development of such a situation. Mr Barrett used every means open to a Victorian father to prevent his daughter from marrying, but a modern parent can also produce the same effect, though in a far less obvious way, and be quite unaware he is doing it. Analytic practice is full of young men and women who have not been weaned from their parents' psyche, and so cannot live like adults. Jung has gone so far as to say that it is little use treating a problem child unless the parents will attempt to clear up their own difficulties at the same time, but followers of his have somewhat modified this point of view, finding that it is possible to develop and strengthen the consciousness of a child so that he can become to some extent an individual able to resist harmful influences.[2]

One practical consequence for parents of this unconscious influence on children is that the personality of the former will have far more effect in shaping the child's character than any precepts; what they say is less important than what they are. This is not a new idea, but rather an example of ancient wisdom strikingly confirmed by modern knowledge.

1. *The Inner World of Childhood*, Frances G. Wickes, pp. 46–7.
2. Cf. *The Life of Childhood*, M.S.M. Fordham, pp. 131, 132.

It follows that parents, and especially parents of so-called 'maladjusted children', even if the maladjustment is only slight, can learn more about themselves and their inner life with great advantage, since the influence of the unknown is so much more harmful than that of the known.

Children often live out some aspect of their parents' personality which has been repressed, or which circumstance has prevented them developing. In the latter case the parents' influence is often conscious or half-conscious, and mistakes it leads to can be seen, at least by other people, if not by themselves; when for example parents say 'We want him to have the education we missed', regardless of whether the kind of education of which they are thinking is suitable for their particular child, and as a result he fails at school or university. When, however, a parent has repressed the sexual instinct it is less apparent why their daughter should be 'man mad', or their son develop into a rake. Somehow (and only the careful and detailed following of a life history will show how this happens) the energy of the repressed unconscious tendency has worked in a thousand ways to push the children into the path of what the parent most fears, and at the same time most desires.

That this unconscious influence can work in a bizarre and terrifying way is shown by T. S. Eliot in *The Family Reunion*. Here the influence is collective rather than personal, and is expressed as a family curse – a fate. Lord Monchensy wanted to kill his wife, but was prevented by his own weakness and the decision of the woman he loved. His son Harry becomes convinced he has acted on the unconscious desire to kill *his* wife by pushing her overboard from the liner on which they are travelling. Harry is pursued by tormenting questions, fears, and fantasies which go far beyond the guilt he might have been expected to feel, and it is only when he returns to his old home that he learns the secret of the past, and is made free by this knowledge to live his own life.

> Perhaps my life has only been a dream
> Dreamt through me by the minds of others

says Harry, while he is trying to understand what has happened to him. In the play T.S.Eliot shows something of the hidden yet powerful influences that had worked on him as the result of his parents' failure to face their own passion and violence:

> Seven years I kept him,
> For the sake of the future, a discontented ghost,
> In his own house ...
> Forcing sons upon an unwilling father

says Harry's mother of her husband:

> I *would* have sons, if I could not have a husband
> Then I let him go.

And Harry says:

> I think the things that are taken for granted at home, make a deeper impression upon children than what they are told.

What is important, if children are to develop satisfactorily, is that their parents should accept life and live it as fully[1] as possible, and when there is frustration, as there often must be, they should be honest with themselves and acknowledge it. It is the secret, hidden things, the skeletons in the cupboard, that harm.

Just as it is vital for parents to live their own lives as fully as possible and to deepen their understanding of themselves to the utmost, so is it important for teachers and educators to do the same. When children go to school their teachers become, during school hours, substitutes for the parents, the children transfer to the teacher some of the feelings they have for their parents and are influenced in their turn by the personalities of the teachers. This mutual relationship is of more importance than any teaching method, and a child's ability to learn is continually hampered if the relationship is unsatisfactory. Again, if teachers really want to be educators, to help children to develop into satisfactory men and

---

1. What is meant here by 'living fully' is the acceptance, rather than the avoidance of experience. For example, there are people who postpone marriage on the grounds that they 'can't afford it', long after this has ceased to be reasonable caution, or others whose lives are paralysed because of the fear of what people will think.

women, and not simply to 'stuff them with knowledge', they will only be really successful if they themselves have sound personalities. No amount of preaching, however well done, no principles, however sound, no clever technique or mechanical aids can replace the influence of a well-developed personality. Teachers cannot expect to be 'whole individuals', in the sense of being individuated, at least, not until they reach middle life or later, but they should live as normally and fully as possible, and extend their knowledge of themselves as far as they can, in order to avoid projecting their complexes on to the children in their care; otherwise they waste their energy and distort the aims of their more impressionable pupils.

The harmful effect of an over-anxious or warped personality is usually clearly seen, and a child can (and usually does) react against such influences, but the projection of a complex is more subtle. For instance, an unmarried woman teacher who has not come to terms with her animus may so overstress the value of intellectual achievement as to leave her girl pupils with a sense of the inferiority of specifically feminine aims which will be a constant difficulty in later life. This will not happen, of course, with those girls who are assured of the value of their femininity, but only when the ground is already prepared by the child's early relationship with her mother having failed to develop satisfactorily.

The complexes of teachers are also much in evidence in the perennial arguments for and against discipline. The infantile teacher who is really incapable of exerting consistent discipline often exalts freedom into a principle, whilst others, urged on by a will to power, or because they have identified themselves with an authoritarian figure, insist on the necessity of the strictest rules and punishments. Such people argue, and even put their ideas into practice without any real consideration of their merits, sometimes with most unfortunate consequences. It is only fair to add that there are of course many teachers who can and do consider these things in an open-minded fashion.

Parents and teachers, because of their influence on future

generations, have the greatest need of a healthy attitude to life and to themselves. One might add that politicians and all who are concerned with people, with making laws or framing policies, would be less likely to make dangerous mistakes if they understood better both their own motives and the dynamics of human nature. At present such knowledge is usually employed negatively – that is, to exploit situations, rather than in positive ways.

Such considerations as these lead Jung to the suggestion that adults are as much in need of education as children, though it is a different kind of education from which the schools give that he has in mind.

At present [Jung says] we educate people only up to the point where they can earn a living and marry; then education ceases altogether, as though a complete mental outfit had been acquired. The solution of all the remaining complicated problems of life is left to the discretion – and ignorance – of the individual. Innumerable ill-advised and unhappy marriages, innumerable professional disappointments, are due solely to this lack of adult education. Vast numbers of men and women thus spend their entire lives in complete ignorance of the most important things.[1]

We have already seen, for instance, how the extravert and the introvert misunderstand each other, and how their personal relationships are complicated by their different attitudes to life. It is clear that some understanding of this basic difference would be helpful, especially to the introvert, who, because of the general popularity of the extraverted attitude, is in danger of feeling inferior, or of being accused of unsociability, egocentricity, and even morbidity, if he or she wants to be alone. Introverts should choose professions which do not force them out of their natural reticence, and work where reflection is more important than quick decisions. Extraverts, on the other hand, should not choose solitary positions, or work where they must be often alone. In spite of the obviousness of this and the fact that most people possess some such knowledge of themselves, it is surprising how

1. *The Development of Personality*, p. 57, 'Child Development and Education'.

often they allow themselves to be forced by circumstance or tradition into an unsuitable position. Husbands and wives might also be more tolerant if they realized they were dealing with something inherent, when their partner's attitude differed from their own.

Some understanding of the effect of the anima and animus is particularly helpful in personal relationships. When, for example, a man makes a startling assumption about a woman, or vice versa, it is because the anima or animus is being projected on to the other person. If the assumption is flattering, no one is likely to object (except the friends and relations who exclaim, 'I can't think what he sees in her'), but when it is critical or derogatory the misunderstood person is usually up in arms. Innumerable quarrels between husband and wife have their basis in this kind of misunderstanding. The moods and emotional outbursts produced in a man by the anima are irrational, and very troublesome to a woman who does not understand them. Some have an instinctive gift for knowing that the mood is best ignored, and that it does not relate to anything they have said or done, others are seized by their own animus and wish to prove that the man is wrong, or that he is behaving unreasonably. Soon an argument develops, they are both plunged into the un·conscious, and anything may happen.

If a man does not realize that he possesses the anima image within himself, he will tend to project it on to women he meets, and, especially if his feeling side is undeveloped, he is easily fascinated. Sometimes circumstances combine to push him literally into the arms of the fascinator, and if he is really possessed, he will throw over everything, even ruin his career, for her sake. This is the theme of so many films and novels as to show what an ever-present factor it is in life. Perhaps the anima projection cannot for the time being be withdrawn, perhaps there is something valuable to the man that he can only realize in this way; but he should understand what it is that possesses him, so that the experience can serve to develop him, and not simply wreck everything that he has hitherto established. Men tend to depreciate feminine qualities, so that it is particularly difficult for them to accept these as also being elements in their own personality. It is only, however, by developing this side of themselves that they can become relatively immune to the more destructive aspects of anima influence. Women, on the other hand, tend to exaggerate the value and importance of male attributes, so that it is flattering to them to develop these in themselves, and they sometimes overdo it, becoming masculine women – that is, women ruled by the animus rather than women who can make use of his qualities to enrich their femininity.

If the animus overrules her a woman will always be making trouble with ill-considered remarks, aggressive behaviour, and obstinate opinions. Women's movements, which always have the driving force of the animus behind them, express the unconscious aspect of women's nature, and often depreciate or forget those feminine qualities which are equally valuable and absolutely necessary to a balanced and healthy life.

The integration of the anima and animus into conscious life – i.e. those aspects of the two archetypes which it is possible to integrate – leads to the possibility of a new kind of relationship between men and women. Instead of each playing complementary roles, they become equal partners. This in some ways demands more of them, for as long as each was content to stick to his part, life might go smoothly, though it was always in danger of disruptive influences from the unconscious. Now they must perhaps concede more to the other, yield up some of their special territory; but they are freer from the disturbingly irrational unconscious, or at least they recognize it for what it is. This development of personality leads to the possibility of a new relationship between man and woman, and in marriage to a partnership that has moved beyond the merely biological, and other aims besides the satisfaction of the sexual instinct and the raising of children can be shared. There are signs that a development of this kind is already fairly widespread; men share feminine tasks in a way that was almost unheard of twenty years ago, and it is not uncommon for women to have interests outside their family, and work outside the home.[1] Such developments, however, have mainly come about through necessity, rather than a conscious wish to extend the personality. It is true that the feminists chose to develop their masculine side, but in doing so they relegated their femininity to the unconscious, so that they simply reversed things instead of widening their consciousness. And because men and women are not fully aware of what they are doing there is always a certain uneasiness about their progress, and a failure of society to keep step.

Unfortunately there is no easy solution of this dilemma, the gap in adult knowledge and awareness cannot be made good by attending a few lectures or reading some books on psychology. Knowledge can even be a hindrance, used as a defence against experience, an excuse for avoiding difficulties which might if accepted lead to a development of personality, or for the justification of a pessimistic attitude to life. How often one has heard people who know a little psychology put all their failures down to the way they were mishandled as children! If they were less blind they would see that this very mishandling could often be the starting point for their own development as individuals, simply because it made dependence on the parents disagreeable – even a smothering affection can produce this reaction against its inhibiting effects. One could cite hosts of famous men and women who triumphed over unhappy childhoods, working their difficulties into the pattern of their lives in such a way that they often became the driving force and material of their success. The history of the great educator Froebel is a striking example of this.

Jung illustrates the limitations of a mere knowledge of psychology with the story of a neurotic young man who came to him with a complete dossier of his case. 'Here', said the young man in effect, 'is the genesis and meaning of my neurosis; why, can you tell me, if I understand myself so

1. There have, of course, always been sections of the community where women's work outside the home has been the rule rather than the exception, but these were special cases, not the general pattern of society.

completely, do my symptoms persist? Why am I not cured?'

In discussion with the young man, it was revealed that though he had very little money, he often spent the winters at St Moritz or in the South. 'How', asked Jung, 'was this possible?' It seemed that a woman friend of his, a not-very-well-off school-teacher, paid for these holidays, and when Jung suggested that this was scarcely a fair arrangement, the young man indignantly countered that they had talked all that over and she was entirely in agreement that he should have these holidays at her expense. He was quite unable to see that he was exploiting the woman's affection for him, and that this egotistical and infantile attitude had something to do with the persistence of his neurosis. People will often accept those weaknesses to which they can attach psychological labels, and thinking they have done all that is necessary, blind themselves to the real nature of their shadow. In fact the most comprehensive knowledge of psychology can leave the personality untouched, and the relationship with an analyst, as well as the will to develop, is often necessary to engender a real change.

Analysis, as a method of education applied to normal people, can only hope to show its effects slowly and in a relatively limited number of cases. Jung as a physician, accustomed to dealing with individuals (using the word here in its ordinary and not in his own specialized sense), is undismayed by this.

All beginnings [he says] are small. We should therefore not mind doing tedious but conscientious work on obscure individuals, even though the goal towards which we strive seems unattainably far off. But one goal we can attain, and that is to develop and bring to maturity individual personalities.[1]

Intellectual knowledge need not be dismissed, however, as useless, especially if it stimulates people, as if often does, to look farther and deeper into themselves; it can also show

1. *The Practice of Psychotherapy*, p. 110, 'Psychotherapy To-day'.

where difficulties are most likely to arise and where development needs to take place. Knowledge can also make people
look again at the things they have taken for granted, and
question them; and it can rouse their sense of values, and
show them that the creative power of the imagination is not
limited to artists and writers. The particular value of analysis is that it demonstrates the unconscious as a force to be
reckoned with, allows its expression in controlled circumstances, and helps to find a channel for the libido if the ordinary ones are closed; it also touches the deep springs of the
religious spirit.

Some knowledge and experience of the collective unconscious is also absolutely necessary, if we are to understand
those forces which have in our time moved vast numbers of
men and women to throw over their civilized standards and
act in a brutal and terrifying way. Nations are made up of
separate men and women and the study of the individual
shows, 'as in a test tube', the forces which move them;
'psychopathology of the masses is rooted in the psychology of
the individual'.[1] But in any large gathering of people it is
not the unique qualities of individuals that count – these
only serve to differentiate, not to unite them – it is rather
what is common to all – namely, the archetypes. When the
same archetype is active in a number of people it draws
them together, as if by magnetic force, and drives them to
act in an irrational way. In addition, a group to preserve its
life must stress the adaptation of each of its members, so that
differences become a disadvantage and average qualities are
cultivated. Hence the larger the group the more stupid it is
likely to become; even a collection of highly intelligent
people will act at a much lower level of intelligence than its
individual members, and Jung once said bitingly that a hundred intelligent heads added up to one hydrocephalus.

In 1928 he wrote:

Our admiration for great organizations dwindles when once
we become aware of the other side of the wonder: the tremendous

1. *Essays on Contemporary Events*, Introduction, p. ix.

piling up and accentuation of all that is primitive in man, and the unavoidable destruction of his individuality in the interests of the monstrosity that every great organization in fact is. The man of today, who resembles more or less the collective ideal, has made his heart into a den of murderers, as can easily be proved by the analysis of his unconscious, even though he himself is not in the least disturbed by it. And in so far as he is normally 'adapted' to his environment, it is true that the greatest infamy on the part of his group will not disturb him, so long as the majority of his fellows steadfastly believe in the exalted morality of their social organization.[1]

These are strong words, but the events that followed showed how sadly right Jung was.

Since the development of applied science in the last hundred years, man's material progress has been rapid, but he has moved dangerously far from his roots in the soil. The taller the tree the deeper its roots should go, but modern man has little relationship with nature, and so has become dangerously unstable and a victim of any storms that blow. In addition, our social organization with its laws – written and unwritten – and its system of education, represses his unconscious instinctive nature and civilizes him outwardly, while leaving what is primitive in him untamed and chafing under the restraint. And as he does not realize how primitive he really is, he becomes like someone who unaware carries dynamite in his pockets disguised as harmless cigarettes. Anything that weakens his repression may loose an outburst of violence, or result in chaotic and disorderly behaviour, in an attempt of the unconscious to compensate for the over-civilized and one-sided conscious attitude.

When life is orderly and disciplined the compensatory unconscious will manifest itself in a chaotic manner, but when disorder rules, as it does to some extent after war, and to a much greater extent during revolutionary periods, the unconscious attempts to compensate by producing symbols of order, and man begins to long for a settled and orderly state of affairs. Instead, however, of realizing that his unconscious

1. *Two Essays on Analytical Psychology*, p. 151.

wish should first be made manifest in his own life, he projects it on to governments and leaders that promise a new order, regardless of how that order is to be obtained, and so he swings from one extreme to the other, motivated and possessed by the archetypes of the unconscious.

If ... a compensatory move of the unconscious is not integrated into consciousness in the case of an individual, it leads to a neurosis or even to a psychosis, and the same would apply to a collectivity. Now there must be something wrong with the conscious attitude for a compensatory move of this kind to be possible; something must be amiss or exaggerated, because only a faulty consciousness can call forth a counter-move on the part of the unconscious. Well, innumerable things have been wrong, as you know, and opinions are thoroughly divided about them. Which is the correct opinion will only be learnt *ex effectu*; that is, we can only discover what the defects in the consciousness of our epoch are by observing the kind of reaction they call forth from the unconscious.[1]

It is this longing for order, and difficulty in tolerating states of tension, that lead men to support totalitarian forms of government which end by enslaving them, and reducing the individual to a mere cog in the machine. On the other hand:

True democracy [as Jung says] is a highly psychological organization, which takes human nature into account as it is, and therefore makes allowance for the need of conflict within its own national frame.[2]

In other words, neither complete anarchy nor complete order are possible while human nature remains much as it is, and the only healthy state of affairs is one which allows for some conflict and disorder, as well as for some order and discipline.

The development of individual consciousness and the integration by the individual of unconscious contents are the only real safeguards against possession by the archetypes, and therefore against dangerous mass movements. An arche-

1. *Essays on Contemporary Events*, Introduction, pp. x–xi.
2. *Ibid.*, p. xvii.

type, like everything unconscious, is two-faced: it can produce completely opposite effects, be either evil or good, destructive or constructive. The aspect it presents depends largely on the conscious attitude, and its effects on the individual's capacity for understanding and moral evaluation.

Now the integration of unconscious contents is an individual act of realization, of understanding, and moral evaluation. It is a most difficult task, demanding a high degree of ethical responsibility. Only relatively few individuals can be expected to be capable of such an accomplishment, and they are not the political but the moral leaders of mankind. The maintenance and further development of civilization depend upon such individuals.[1]

But even if there are only a few individuals capable of such development, the rest are not excused from making the attempt. It is, in fact, clear that everyone, even if only for his own safety, should make some effort to realize and understand the unconscious.

1. *Essays on Contemporary Events*, Introduction, p. xii.

Glossary

affect: emotion (see p. 23)

anima: the unconscious feminine side of a man (see pp. 52-5)

animus: the unconscious masculine side of a woman (see pp. 55-8)

archetype: a content of the collective unconscious which is the psychological counterpart of instinct. Also loosely used to designate a
collective image or symbol (see pp. 24, 25)

collective: psychic contents which are not common to one individual,
but to many. When these are unconscious they are termed the
collective unconscious (see pp. 22, 23)

complex: an affectively toned group of associated ideas (see p. 23)

cryptomnesia: something seen, heard, or read and forgotten and then
later reproduced without consciousness of its source (see p. 25)

ego: the centre of the conscious mind (see p. 21)

enantiodromia: the view that everything eventually goes over into its
opposite (see p. 18)

extraversion: the turning of the libido towards outer objects (see p. 29)

fantasy: imaginative activity (see p. 27)

hydrocephalus: the distension of the brain cavities by the accumulation of fluid, resulting in an enlargement of the skull (see p. 18)

individual: the integrated whole personality (see p. 71)

individuation: the process of becoming an individual (see pp. 76-83)

instinct: an unconsciously determined impulse, or action which is
collective (see pp. 23, 24)

introversion: the turning of the libido towards inner objects (see
p. 29)

libido: psychic energy (see pp. 17-20)

neurosis: a disorder of the psyche caused by unconscious conflict, in
which the ego remains relatively intact (see pp. 84-9)

participation mystique: Lévy-Bruhl's term for a peculiar kind of
psychological connexion with the object, where the subject is
unable to differentiate himself clearly from it (see p. 27)

persona: the facet of personality which is turned to the world and by
which a relationship with the environment is made (see
pp. 47-9)

personal unconscious: repressed memories, wishes, emotions, &c., and
subliminal perceptions of a personal nature (see pp. 22, 47)

projection: the transmitting of a subjective process into an object
(see p. 53)

Glossary

psyche: a necessary postulate defining the subject matter of psychology, and as such including the conscious and the unconscious (see pp. 15–17)

psychic: pertaining to the psyche (see p. 15)

psychosis: the invasion of the conscious by unconscious contents, so that the ego is partially or completely overwhelmed. What is commonly known as insanity (see p. 19)

reductive analysis: the reduction of or tracing back of psychic manifestations to their original source (see p. 106)

repression: the more or less deliberate withdrawal of attention from some disagreeable experience, causing it to be expelled from consciousness so that it cannot be recalled at will (see p. 21)

schizoid: a split personality, an introverted personality which is not, however, insane (see p. 41)

self: the centre of the totality of ego and unconscious, and/or the synthesis of ego and unconscious (see pp. 61–5)

shadow: the unconscious 'natural' side of a human being (see pp. 49–52)

symbol: an expression of something relatively unknown which cannot be conveyed in any other way (see p. 20)

trauma: psychic injury (see p. 85)

> The above terms are defined in the sense in which they are generally used by Jung, as his usage sometimes differs slightly from the ordinary, or from that of other psychologists.

Bibliography

of the Principal Translated Works of C. G. Jung

The Psychology of the Unconscious. New York 1916, London 1917
A technical work containing a wealth of mythological material.
It marks the period of transition when Jung's work was diverging
from that of Freud. This book has recently been revised by the
author and published as 'Wandlungen und Symbole der Libido'.
It has appeared in the 'Collected Works' as *Symbols of Transformation*

Studies in Word Association. London 1918
A technical volume containing studies by Jung and others

Psychological Types. London 1923
The 'types' described in detail, and their different manifestations in history, literature, philosophy, aesthetics, psychiatry, &c.

Contributions to Analytical Psychology. London & New York 1928
Essays and Lectures, some technical (e.g. 'On Psychic Energy'),
many of general interest

Two Essays on Analytical Psychology. London 1953 (Coll. Wks, vol. 7)
The best introduction to Analytical Psychology

The Secret of the Golden Flower. London 1931
The study of a Chinese Yoga text by Richard Wilhelm, with a
commentary by C. G. Jung, drawing comparisons with the European way of individuation

Modern Man in Search of a Soul. London 1933
Essays and lectures of general interest

Psychology and Religion. London 1958 (Coll. Wks, vol. 11)
Lectures given at Yale University, and of technical and general
interest

The Integration of the Personality. New York 1939. London 1940
A study in the individuation process and an introduction to later
work on the symbolism of alchemy – of general interest

Essays on Contemporary Events. London 1947
A short collection of essays, lectures, and one broadcast talk,
chiefly concerned with problems arising out of the war, and of
general interest

Bibliography

Introduction to a Science of Mythology. London 1949, or the same
  translation, New York 1949 published as *Essays on a Science of
  Mythology* (in collaboration with C. Kerényi)
  A parallel study of mythology and two archetypes of the collective unconscious. Somewhat difficult to read, but nevertheless of
  general interest

Psychology and Alchemy. London 1953 (Coll. Wks, vol. 12)
  A study of alchemical symbolism, illustrated by material from
  400 dreams. This book, which is largely technical, is an introduction to all Jung's later work

Collected Works
  Refers to the edition of Professor Jung's complete works, published under the auspices of the Bollingen Foundation, New
  York, by Pantheon Books in the United States and Routledge in
  England. In this new edition many of the papers, essays, &c.,
  have been re-grouped and appear in different volumes from
  those of their original publication. Previously untranslated works
  are also included

The Practice of Psychotherapy (Coll. Wks 16)

The Development of Personality (Coll. Wks 17)

Aion (Coll. Wks, vol. 9: pt 2)

The Archetypes and the Collective Unconscious (Coll. Wks, vol. 9: pt 1)

Index

Active imagination, 66
Adler, Alfred, 30, 84, 85, 91
Aion, 53, 55
Alchemy, 80, 81, 95
Analytical psychology, 84
Anima, animus, 28, 52 ff., 114, 115
Aquinas, Thomas, 81
Archetypes, 24, 25, 27, 28
Archetypes and the Collective Unconscious, The, 54, 55, 73, 77, 80
Association tests, 22, 108

Basis of Jung's psychology, 15
Before Philosophy, 27
Blake, William, 45
Bowen, Elizabeth: *The Death of the Heart*, 49
Boyle, Robert, 81
Buddha, The, 64
Buddhism, Feeling an important element in, 40
Burckhardt, Jacob, 24

Christ, 64
Christian civilization, Hollowness of, 74
Christianity, Feeling an important element in, 40
Collected Papers on Analytical Psychology, 108
Collective unconscious, 22, 23, 25, 27, 28, 49
Compensatory unconscious, Manifestations of the, 119, 120
Complex psychology, 84
Complexes, 23
Concealment, 89, 90
Confession, 89 ff.

Contributions to Analytical Psychology, 19, 22, 23, 24, 26, 28, 31, 92, 113
Crashaw, Richard: *Upon the Book and Picture of the Seraphical Saint Teresa*, 104
Cryptomnesia, 25

Darwin, Charles, 36
Development of the Personality, The, 83, 105
Donne, John: *Devotions upon Emergent Occasions*, 78
Dreams, 25, 58, 75, 85
  Ancient man's view of, 102
  As warnings of danger, 104
  Collective, 99, 100
  Compensatory in character, 103
  Conflicts revealed by, 103
  Definition of, 97
  Dreamt by members of the same family, 105
  Modern popular views of, 102
  Of children, reflecting parents' problems, 105, 108
  Personal, 99, 100
  Prospective, 104
  Recalling events, 105
  To be taken seriously, 97
  Understanding of, 97
  Wish-revealing, 104
Dynamism of the religious function, 71

Earth mother (*see also* Great mother), 28
Ego, The, 21, 62
Eliot, T. S.: *The Family Reunion*, 110
Emotion, Concealment of, 90
Enantiodromia, Law of, 18

126

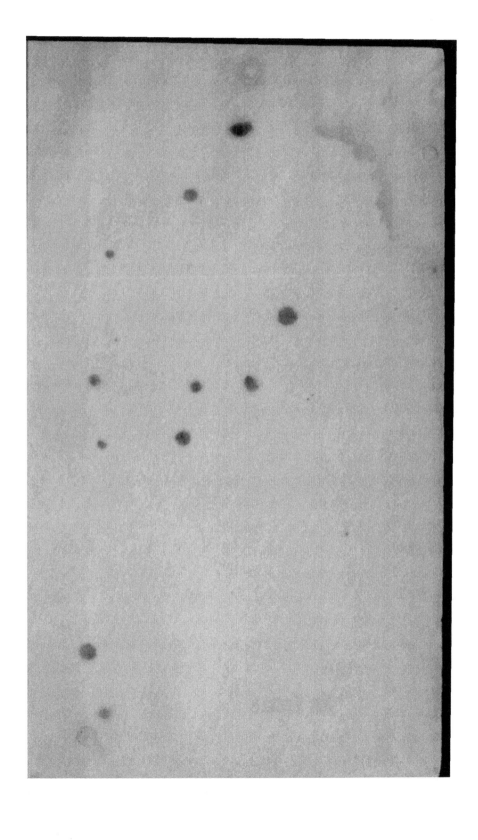